T. Moros

Andrew Davies has taught widely in adult education and currently works for the Extra Mural Departments at Cambridge and London Universities, the City University, and the Workers' Educational Association. He is also the author of two forthcoming books, on the people's London and popular drama in Britain. Born in 1955, Andrew Davies lives in London.

D1586126

Andrew Davies

Where did the Forties go?

A popular history

Pluto Press

London and Sydney

First published in 1984 by Pluto Press Limited,
The Works, 105a Torriano Avenue, London NW5 2RX
and Pluto Press Australia Limited, PO Box 199,
Leichhardt, New South Wales 2040, Australia

Copyright © Andrew Davies, 1984

Cover designed by Clive Challis A. Gr. R.
Set by Grassroots Typeset, London NW6
Printed in Great Britain by Photobooks (Bristol) Limited
Bound by W.H.Ware & Sons Limited, Tweed Road,
Clevedon, Avon

British Library Cataloguing in Publication Data
Davies, Andrew
   Where did the forties go?
   1. Europe—History—1918—1945   2. Europe
   —History—1945—
   I. Title
   940.53   D424

ISBN 0-86104-758-3

Contents

Preface

' "It's a poor sort of memory that only works backwards", the Queen remarked.'

This passage from Lewis Carroll's *Through the Looking Glass*, published in 1872, came into my mind when I read the findings of a poll reported in the *Sunday Times* of 25 May 1980. Students and pupils were asked questions about the Second World War: 'Most young people do not know who won at El Alamein, or what the Battle of Britain was, or what Rommel or Mussolini did.' One third of the interviewees thought the British had won at Dunkirk.

This started me thinking about the 1940s, a period resonant with images and myths: the Blitz and the Battle of Britain, Churchill in his boiler-suit, puffing away at a cigar and winning the war, Hiroshima and Nagasaki, the sinister Iron Curtain. And strangely enough the war remained a particularly lively 'memory' for those millions of people, like myself, born since 1945 but brought up on war comics, novels, and films such as *The Dambusters*, *The Bridge Over the River Kwai* and *Reach for the Sky*.

Although I came across the *Beyond the Fringe* scripts written in the early 1960s that had parodied the patriotic nostalgia with which the war was often recalled, I could not find much material on what had actually happened in the 1940s — unlike 'the Thirties', which seemed a pretty well-tilled area.

So, where did the Forties go? One reason for their dis-appearance lies in the proclivity of historians for neat categories — so that the war means a book ending in 1945 or the Attlee govern-ments, a book covering the years 1945—51. However I think that there are reasons for looking at the 1940s as a whole, although it is not a case of swapping one generalization for another—this book spills over into both the 1930s and the entire postwar period.

Where did the Forties go? is something more than a 'history'; one theme running throughout is the way our memories of past events—even if we have no first-hand experience of them—can influence the present and the future. Another theme explores the tramlines constructed in the 1940s which have shaped, and continue to shape, people's lives. Although the decade witnessed some terrible tragedies and atrocities, it also saw resilience, courage and idealism. Maybe the sense of opportunity present in the early 1940s was later turned in upon itself; yet the fact that it existed at all gives cause for hope.

But Shelley put it better in the closing lines of *Prometheus Unbound*:

> To suffer woes which Hope thinks infinite;
> To forgive wrongs darker than death or night;
> To defy Power, which seems omnipotent:
> To love and bear; to hope till Hope creates
> From its own wreck the thing it contemplates;
> Neither to change, nor falter, nor repent;
> This, like thy glory, Titan! is to be
> Good, great and joyous, beautiful and free;
> This is alone Life, Joy, Empire and Victory.

Acknowledgements

Many people have helped with this book over several years. Versions of it have been presented at conferences, seminars, extramural and WEA classes and I would like to thank everyone for their thoughtful reactions.

In particular, I am very grateful to: Simon Blanchard; Paul Crane; Basil Davidson; Emma Davies; Simon and Julia Davies; Jo Florent; Michael Kidron; Richard Kuper; Liz McGuirk; and all those at 37a Clerkenwell Green.

Finally, my parents have been unstinting with their love and support, and Jean has provided help, encouragement and much else in the last frantic months when the manuscript was being typed and we were also trying to move flat.

1 December 1983

Key dates

30 January 1933 Hitler becomes Chancellor of Germany.
July 1936 Republican government in Spain attacked by
    Franco's Nationalists.
23 August 1939 Nazi-Soviet Pact.
3 September 1939 Britain declares war on Germany.
April 1940 German offensive launched.
10 May 1940 Churchill replaces Chamberlain as Prime
    Minister.
26 May 1940 The evacuation from Dunkirk begins.
14 June 1940 German occupation of Paris.
7 September 1940 Beginning of the Blitz.
22 June 1941 German attack on Soviet Union.
December 1942 Publication of the Beveridge Report.
January 1943 Surrender of German forces after the Battle of
    Stalingrad.
6 June 1944 D-Day.
July 1944 Bretton Woods Conference sets up the IMF and
    World Bank.
October 1944 Stalin—Churchill 'percentage agreement' in
    Moscow.
December 1944 British troops intervene in Greece.
13—14 February 1945 Terror raid on Dresden.
12 April 1945 Death of Roosevelt—Truman becomes
    President of The United States.
April 1945 American and Soviet troops meet on the Elbe.
7 May 1945 German surrender.
July 1945 Labour Party wins general election by a large
    majority.

6 & 9 August 1945 Atom bombs dropped on Hiroshima and Nagasaki.

August 1945 The Potsdam Agreement.

October 1945 French Constituent Assembly elections – the Communist Party wins most votes.

March 1946 Churchill's 'iron curtain' speech in Fulton, Missouri.

January 1947 'Bizonia' – fusion of American and British zones in Germany.

March 1947 Pronouncement of 'the Truman doctrine'.

May 1947 Communists ousted from the French government.

June 1947 Communists ousted from the Italian government.

June 1947 Marshall Aid plan announced.

August 1947 British withdrawal from India.

October 1947 Cominform (Communist Information Bureau) set up.

February 1948 Communists seize power in Czechoslovakia.

April 1948 Christian Democrat success in Italian general election.

June 1948 Start of the Berlin airlift.

June 1948 USSR – Yugoslav break.

June 1948 Introduction of American bases to Britain.

July 1948 the National Health Service begins.

April 1949 Founding of NATO (North Atlantic Treaty Organization).

September 1949 Proclamation of People's Republic of China.

September 1949 Establishment of Federal Republic of Germany (West Germany).

October 1949 Establishment of German Democratic Republic (East Germany).

October 1949 Cuts in education, housing and health budgets in Britain.

June 1950 Start of the Korean War.

1. All our yesterdays?

In Marcel Ophuls's film *The Sorrow and the Pity*, made in 1970, a succession of French people are asked about their lives under German occupation during the Second World War. Many of them claim to have helped the Resistance. Sadly, newspapers of the time tell a very different story, of these same people's activities as collaborators and informers. What Daddy did in the war had become what he now, with hindsight, would like to have done.

This is a graphic example of the frailties of human memory, of time obscuring and altering unpleasant events. Similarly, autobiographies are notorious for their tendency to exaggerate the subject's own importance or to gloss over particular episodes.

However vaguely it is recalled, the power of the past is of vital significance. People's actions and thoughts are rooted in their memories and interpretations of what has gone before. Attitudes towards members of one's family, friends, neighbours and enemies are heavily conditioned by how one has got on with them before now, and arguments often focus on the clash between different views of the 'same' events.

Memories and historical judgements are by their very nature selective and partial—especially when something critical is at stake. Frequently the memory emphasizes certain aspects of past events in order to reinforce contemporary beliefs and aspirations. The marchers of the Orange Lodges in Belfast are adorned with regalia and mementos which serve to remind both onlookers and participants of the supposed wickedness of Catholics in general, and in particular of the victory of William of Orange at the Battle of the Boyne in 1690. This display has an objective in the here and now: to stiffen Protestant resolve in the face of proposals for a united Ireland. Similarly at Scotland *v* England football matches, Scottish fans often carry banners with the figures '1314' on them, the year the Scots defeated the English at Bannockburn. In China today statues of Mao Tse-Tung are being demolished because many of the former leader's ideas clash with current policies—these are memories that must be erased if at all possible.

The last example brings out the point that popular memory is never a fixed or monolithic object, but rather a flux of often contradictory views. Memories invariably require 'topping up': otherwise, like names and telephone numbers, they have a habit of disappearing.

The available psychological research on this question often omits discussion of specific, concrete cases, and the tendency of much academic work is to approach such topics in rather a rationalist fashion—as if people draw up a detailed balance-sheet before deciding what to do next. Three examples from the 1940s—concerning Churchill, Dunkirk and Orwell's *1984*—indicate just how certain events can be imbued with a power which enables them to exercise a lasting influence.

Leaders are often deified during wartime in order to bolster morale, and no doubt tales of Hitler's omniscience and infallibility shored up German efforts just as in the Soviet Union Stalin was projected as the living symbol of Soviet determination. In Britain, once Chamberlain had been replaced by Churchill as prime minister in May 1940, a similar effort was set in motion, albeit often unconsciously. 'Good old Winnie' with his cigars and boiler-suits, the implacable speeches full of defiance and resolve, became the embodiment of 'the bulldog spirit'.

The Conservative Party played upon this identification as much as possible; for instance their manifesto for the 1945 general election was entitled simply *Mr Churchill's Declaration of Policy to the Electors*. Churchill himself did nothing to diminish the 'superman' legend with the publication, from 1948, of his six-volume *History of the Second World War*. There the image he chose to emphasize was that of 'the man of destiny'. As he phrased it when he became prime minister in 1940: 'I felt as if I was walking with destiny, and that all my past life had been but a preparation for this hour and for this trial.'[1] This theme was taken up by subsequent commentators. For example Isaiah Berlin, in his much reprinted article 'Mr Churchill' which first appeared in 1949, concluded that Churchill was 'a legendary hero who belongs to myth as much as to reality'.[2] The potency of this legend was reinforced by Churchill's state funeral in 1965, and is witnessed today by the often-voiced remark that 'Churchill won the war', especially by those born after 1945.

Dunkirk is another event which was embellished with fabrication and myth, again partly for reasons of morale. A badly equipped and incompetently led British expeditionary force was no match for the blitzkrieg tactics of the Germans, and, cornered in Dunkirk, thousands of soldiers had to be evacuated back to England. The defeat was, however, quickly turned into a victory; the *Daily Mirror* editorial summing it all up as 'bloody marvellous'.

The government was also soon in on the act with the publication of two semi-official books that year, Gordon Beccles's *Dunkirk and After* and Gun Buster's *Return via Dunkirk*. In fact there were no newspaper correspondents at all at Dunkirk, and the numerous stories about officers panicking and ditching their men were censored. With the result that, as the *Sunday Times* survey indicated, many young people think the British must have defeated the Germans at Dunkirk.

Superimposed on this saga was the fiction that it was the little boats and tugs which were gallantly taking most of the men off the Dunkirk beaches; or, as J.B.Priestley put it at the time in one of his immensely popular *Postscripts* talks on the radio, 'the little holiday steamers went to hell—and came back glorious.'

Whilst not detracting in any way from the courage of those sailing in small vessels to Dunkirk, the offical figures reveal that the great majority of those evacuated were transported by Royal and French Navy vessels. But once a myth such as this is established, and reinforced by various means—for example, William Wyler's immensely popular film *Mrs Miniver* (1942) and Paul Gallico's story 'The Snow Goose' (1941), both made use of the 'little boats' legend—it is very difficult to overthrow, and attempts to do so are often counterproductive.[3]

Much of the radicalism of the war years has also been discreetly forgotten, that populist upsurge which accompanied an anti-fascist war and rebelled against a return to the reactionary governments and injustices of the interwar period. One important explanation for this lies in the change of mood initiated by the onset of the Cold War from the late 1940s. As Ken Worpole has noted, the wave of books about the war published subsequently — from *The Colditz Story* to the novels of Alistair MacLean — has tended to reproduce the conventions of the adventure story, the heroics and the personalities, at the expense of the social and political background.[4] But in other cases, most notably Geroge Orwell's *1984*, certain interpretations were deliberately played up for contemporary 'Cold War' purposes.

Published in 1949 when Orwell was slowly dying, the book was seized upon by many critics and reviewers, especially in the United States, as a comprehensive and sweeping rejection of socialism. In fact Orwell, as his biographer Bernard Crick has shown, was disturbed by such distortions, writing that:

> My recent novel is NOT intended as an attack on Socialism or on the British Labour Party (of which I am a supporter) but as a show-up of the perversions to which a centralized economy is liable and which have already been partly realized in communism and fascism.[5]

But whatever Orwell's intentions, the Cold War climate ensured that *1984* would be dragged in to denigrate labour movements everywhere.

The effects of the Cold War, although coming after the 1940s, have meant that to study this decade has entailed a vast leap of imagination. Mrs Churchill sponsoring an 'aid to Russia' fund? Conservative MPs praising the wisdom and diplomacy of Marshall Stalin, the ideas of Lenin studied in British schools? The people of Warsaw and Paris, London and Bucharest, Moscow and Rome seeing themselves as participants in a common struggle, the American and Soviet governments jointly putting forward constructive plans and proposals — surely there must be some mistake? But no, it all happened, and yet the Cold War has 'changed' whole chunks of history before its time.

For myself, having been born in the mid-1950s at a period

when the Cold War was already taken for granted, I cannot remember when mention of 'Russia' did not carry with it scarey and menacing overtones. At school we somehow instinctively knew that America was the home of Hollywood and Coca-Cola, where John Wayne righted wrong and everyone drove around in huge cars, spoke in a drawl and was immensely rich. On the other hand Russia was populated by a grim and unsmiling mass, where everyone spied on everyone else and tirelessly plotted the downfall of the West. Some kind of 'iron curtain' – this I had real problems in visualizing – separated 'us' from 'them', the goodies from the baddies.

How do such simplistic pictures come to be constructed? One factor which surfaces in the examples of Churchill, Dunkirk and Orwell is the power of the media. Perhaps in earlier centuries it was the pulpit or the theatre that was crucial in forming opinion, but today even education would seem to have been left behind by television, newspapers, films and radio. The average person in Britain apparently watches between 16 and 20 hours of television a week, and a recent survey found that schoolchildren spend more hours in front of the television than they do in class.

The genre of television history is immensely popular, with series like *The British Empire, Edward VII, The Great War* and *America* attracting huge audiences and winning prizes at international festivals. All the series are lavishly mounted, making full use of the visual qualities of the medium, with well-known performers in the main parts or prestigious figures presenting the less fictionalized programmes. However, they all take place within a context dominated by the search for competitive audience figures, and this requirement for history as entertainment often means that series will be disfigured and trivialized by the ostentatious costumes and sets or an array of gadgets (J.K.Galbraith's *The Age of Uncertainty* provided a good example of this last defect).

The overall style of the programmes usually bears out the dictum of Thomas Carlyle that 'history is the biography of great men', and everything is accordingly reduced to the clash of a few personalities. This cavalier attitude is paralleled by the quality of the criticism the series will receive. History books undergo a gauntlet of reviews that grill them for errors of fact and interpretation, but televised history programmes avoid this process, and television criticism in general is written in a deliberately humorous and superficial manner.

Obviously the press is mainly concerned with present occurrences. Yet editorials and feature articles frequently flesh out the paper's views by reference to historical events, and in this way play some part in the formation of popular memory. The role of the tabloids in perpetuating the stance of the Cold War has been seen in recent years by the rash of 'Red' Kens, Teds or whatever that frequently appear in their headlines.

Together the press and television are extremely influential in forming opinions and views on past events, and in particular it is invariably what they do not print that matters. This problem of what is omitted also crops up with regard to the 1940s. During the war censorship was imposed in order not to reveal anything useful to the enemy, and to maintain morale. The image assiduously promoted was one of 'a nation at war', a country steadfastly united in the common struggle against the enemy, and embarrassing material or information which the public was deemed incapable of interpreting correctly – such as the details about the fall of Singapore and the Dresden bombings – was censored.

Any account of the 1940s has to deal with this difficulty, together with the vast amount of material available from that decade. This book started as a study of just Britain in the 1940s, but again and again I found myself having to widen my horizons to get to grips with the subject. Finally I realized that I should have been looking down the other end of the telescope, that events in Britain at this time could be understood only as part of a wider internationalist whole.

The remaining chapters highlight certain themes and topics. Chapter 2 looks at the years leading up to the outbreak of the Second World War, both in Britain and Europe. Chapter 3 deals with the war years in Britain, especially the shifts in people's moods and opinions. Chapter 4 concerns the initial victories of Nazi Germany and the gradual swell of anti-fascist reaction, focusing particularly on the Resistance and the Soviet contribution to the war. Chapter 5 summarizes the state of Europe in 1945–6, a badly-damaged continent embarking on far-reaching reconstruction programmes – yet with storm-clouds in the offing. Chapter 6 looks at Britain under a Labour government from 1945 to 1951, and the next chapter examines the power and influence of the United States and its part in the making of 'Western' Europe. Chapter 8 considers the role of the Soviet Union in the postwar period and developments in 'Eastern' Europe. Chapter 9 concentrates on the coming of the Cold War and the crucial importance of events in Germany. Chapter 10 summarizes the situation in Europe since the 1950s and links up the 1980s with the 1940s.

One characteristic of the 1940s was that writers produced their work for the general reader—it was at this time that G.M.Trevelyan published his *English Social History*—and I hope that my book will interest those who lived through it as well as those who didn't. There is a guide to further reading at the end for anyone wishing to delve deeper, and the references are to show the inquisitive or sceptical my sources. They contain no further information, so there is no compelling reason to keep flicking from front to back.

2. Britain and Europe in the Thirties

Britain

The 1930s is a period full of images which tug at and jostle the memory, whether they be of Hitler and Mussolini haranguing mass rallies, of unemployment and means test, Chamberlain flying to see Hitler, the Moscow Trials or even the abdication of Edward VIII. Much of the romantic haze which surrounds the decade centres on expressions of resistance—the Hunger Marches and Jarrow, the Battle of Cable Street against Mosley's fascists, British people fighting in the Spanish Civil War—but emphasis on these events can distort the overall picture.

In fact 'the Thirties' was a time of defeat and failure. By 1939 Hitler and Mussolini were entrenched in power, Franco had almost won in Spain, Chamberlain was busy with his policy of appeasement and the dole queues remained alongside the means test.

The year 1930 had begun with a Labour government under Ramsay MacDonald in office, the second in British history. The first Labour government had come to power in 1924 after an election campaign full of Conservative warnings that a vote for Labour was a step on the road towards anarchy, the nationalization of savings and compulsory free love. As it turned out, this short-lived administration managed to do little except demonstrate that such prophecies were wildly inaccurate.

The Labour government which took over from the Conservatives in 1929 soon found itself embroiled in economic crisis. The Wall Street crash occurred in October 1929 and, with stocks and shares plummeting as fast as the bankers hurling themselves out of windows, it triggered off a world-wide recession. Unemployment spiralled upwards everywhere, and nowhere more so than in Britain, where more than two-and-a-half million people were out of work by August 1931.

Faced with this crisis, the Labour government desperately implemented the advice which it was receiving from Whitehall: that a diet of balanced budgets and reduced spending would soon do the trick. In fact, of course, it merely exacerbated the situation. Oswald Mosley, a junior minister in the administration, put forward some innovative proposals in a memorandum of 1930 which argued for a policy of expansion combined with tariffs and import controls; but they were rejected outright by Philip Snowden, the Chancellor of the Exchequer.

By the summer of 1931 the government had resolved on further economies with cuts in the pay of teachers, civil servants, the police and in unemployment benefit. This last plan was too much for the Trades Union Congress (TUC), and in August 1931 MacDonald jettisoned the Labour Party, becoming the leader of a 'National' government comprising many Conservatives and Liberals. At the general election in October, the Conservatives and their associates won 521 seats, the Labour Party a mere 52.

The first responses to this debacle—at the Labour Party conference of 1932—took the form of much angry rhetoric concerning the timidity of the MacDonald government. Clement Attlee for example, who was to be the leader of the party within three years, warned that no further progress could be made in seeking to get crumbs from the rich man's table: 'Whenever we try to do anything,' he said, 'we will be opposed by every vested world interest, financial, political and social.'[1]

But despite much posturing, it is notable just how little change followed in the wake of the 1931 catastrophe. The composition of the labour movement's two most influential bodies—the Labour Party's National Executive Committee (NEC) and the TUC General Council—remained similar to pre-1931 days. Throughout the 1930s the NEC was controlled by Hugh Dalton and Herbert Morrison, the General Council by Ernest Bevin and Walter Citrine; all four were firmly on the right wing of the Labour Party, and their explanations of '1931' were based not on the demerits or otherwise of the government's policies but rather on the personal flaws and corruption of MacDonald himself.

The caution these bodies displayed during the 1930s was paralleled by that of the Parliamentary Labour Party (PLP). Reduced to a rump after 1931, their number was increased to 154 MPs in the 1935 election. However, it was a collection of rather elderly individuals — only eight of them were under 40 years of age — and Aneurin Bevan was one of the few determined that the struggles outside parliament should not be completely muffled by constitutional proprieties. But all in all, it can hardly be claimed that the NEC, TUC or PLP gave much of a lead on three of the vital social and political questions of the period: unemployment, Mosley and his fascists, and the Spanish Civil War.

The numbers of those out of work remained high throughout the decade — there were still over two million jobless in 1935 — and the hardship of unemployment was aggravated by the imposition of a means test in 1931. This took into account the earnings of all members of the household and often meant, for example, that a father's benefit would be cut because a daughter might have a job and so theoretically was supporting the rest of her family. Many families broke up under such tensions.

The reaction of the General Council of the TUC to this state of affairs was somewhat tentative. They circularized local trades councils and asked them to create unemployment associations which they then supplied with footballs and chessboards. Resolutions of protest were sent to MPs and the press, but the TUC drew back from organizing any rallies, marches or demonstrations. Even more, they positively discouraged the unemployed from adopting any attitude other than that of suffering in silence and worked to hinder the activities of the National Unemployed Workers' Movement (NUWM).

Led by a particularly able member of the Communist Party, Wal Hannington, the NUWM had been active since 1921 but it was in the 1930s that it really came into prominence, mainly through its organization of the Hunger Marches. These took place in 1930, 1932, 1934 and 1936, bringing many men and women tramping from their home communities to London in order to protest against a National government which had simply turned its back on them. It took great courage to go on one of the Hunger

Marches because of the considerable hardship entailed. The public assistance committees withdrew dole money from the marchers as they were deemed 'unavailable for work', although of course there was none, and the mounted police were never slow to demonstrate their prowess at baton charges.

On one occasion this agitation was effective. The Unemployment Act of 1934, introduced by Neville Chamberlain, created unemployment assistance boards which were to replace the public assistance committees; more importantly the act also provided for reductions in the scale of relief payments. The ensuing furore was led by the NUWM and the South Wales Miners' Federation, and in February 1935 the government retreated by deciding not to introduce these new reduced levels of payment. Generally, however, it was safely cushioned by its huge parliamentary majority.

The hostility of TUC and Labour Party officials to the Hunger Marches was also revealed in other more petty and vindictive ways. Both in 1930 and 1932 local Labour Parties and trades councils were specifically told not to provide assistance, and Labour Party organizers were sent off along the planned route a few days ahead of the marchers in order to reiterate this instruction. Even the famous Jarrow Crusade of 1936, led by the town's Labour MP Ellen Wilkinson, did not meet with approval, with the result that in Chesterfield provisions and bedding were supplied by the local branch of the Conservatives and not the Labour Party.

Another issue of crucial importance during the 1930s was the rise of Oswald Mosley and his organization the British Union of Fascists, founded in 1932. Since the rejection of his 1930 memorandum, Mosley had moved rapidly to the right and now modelled his party on that of Hitler's Nazis. The BUF headquarters in London's King's Road were transformed into a barracks, members wore blackshirts and gave fascist salutes. British fascism was powerfully assisted by certain newspapers; the headlines for just two of the *Daily Mail* leading articles in January 1934 were 'Put the Nation into Blackshirts' and 'Give the Fascists a Helping Hand', and the *Sunday Dispatch* gave prizes for the best postcards on 'Why I like the Blackshirts'. By 1934 there were 400 branches of the BUF throughout the country with a total membership of over 20,000.

The Labour Party's attitude towards Mosley and fascism was hostile but passive. Pamphlets were published, lectures given, Mosley denounced, but their leaders shied away from actually confronting the BUF on the streets where the physical attacks on Jews took place. Herbert Morrison, the organizer of the London Labour Party, called a conference in September 1934 to discuss the problem of fascists in the East End; doubtless the arguments and debates were both useful and interesting but the conference itself, despite the pleas of some delegates, led to no further action.

In October 1936 word went around that the BUF was to hold a massive anti-semitic demonstration through the East End of London. The Labour Party's advice was to stay at home that day, which in effect meant allowing Mosley and his supporters to march where they pleased. This advice was almost totally disregarded as thousands of men and women thronged the streets and by sheer weight of numbers prevented the BUF march from taking place. The Battle of Cable Street, combined with the Public Order Act of 1936 which prohibited paramilitary activity, and also the partial decline in unemployment, ensured that by the end of the year the BUF was a spent force.

Another major issue of the 1930s was the outbreak of the Spanish Civil War in 1936. During February of that year a Republican government was elected to power which began to introduce certain measures of social reform. This legislation sparked off unrest within the army and in July 1936 the National forces, led by Franco, started a civil war. The legality (if nothing else) of the Republicans failed to sway the 1936 Labour Party and TUC conferences, and they both came out in favour of non-intervention, the same policy as Baldwin's National government.

The Western powers set up a non-intervention committee, which included representatives from France, Italy and Germany, in order to ensure that no foreign forces should intervene in the civil war. But the meetings of this committee soon became a farce when it was widely known that German and Italian troops were aiding Franco's side and still the British and French delegates continued to turn a blind eye to such revelations. Echoing this pusillanimity, throughout the three years of the war neither the General Council of the TUC nor the NEC came out in support of the Republican government. There were of course the occasional gestures; Attlee, for instance, visited British volunteers fighting in Spain just as he had spoken on the platform at the last Hunger March when it reached Hyde Park in 1936.

Well over 2,000 British men and women volunteered to go and help the Republicans in Spain, and the great majority came from working-class homes — although the prominence given to the activities of such writers as George Orwell and W.H.Auden has obscured this fact. Casualties mounted appallingly, and by the time the British volunteers were pulled out of Spain in December 1938 over 500 had been killed and another thousand badly injured. The organization that provided the means by which many people reached Spain, and was also behind many political initiatives of the 1930s, was the Communist Party.

Formed in 1920, the Communist Party of Great Britain had never possessed more than a few thousand members, although the energy and commitment of these individuals enabled the party to wield an influence quite disproportionate to its size. At the beginning of the 1930s the Communist Party was on the wane because of its attempt to carry out the 'class v class' approach of the Communist International in Moscow; stripped of its jargon, this meant that communist parties were to concentrate much of their attack on other parties of the labour movement as being 'social fascists'.

From the mid-1930s the Communist International switched from its 'class v class' line towards an emphasis on popular fronts — broad alliances of all progressive individuals and bodies — but the earlier period left a lasting legacy of bitterness that explains why many people distrusted the communists. However, it remained undeniable that on many issues in the 1930s it was members of the Communist Party who provided the dynamism behind those attempts to break away from much of the seeming apathy of the official labour movement — for example, the NUWM and the British volunteers in Spain.

Although heroic and determined, events like the Hunger Marches, Cable Street and support for the Spanish Republicans amounted to little more than brave gestures in the face of an implacable government. Why was the labour movement so impotent in the 1930s? The standard answer is to blame the leaders of the Labour Party and trade unions for their timidity and failure to give a lead—or, in stronger language, their 'betrayal' of the jobless and low-paid. Certainly as we have seen, men like Citrine and Morrison confined themselves to tame orthodoxies, but in fact there were more important, long-term factors also at work.

One reason was the very existence of widescale poverty and unemployment. Again and again it has been thought that such circumstances would prompt militant action, yet in the Britain of the 1930s (and the 1980s) it inhibited responses, making people fearful of losing their jobs and often plunging them into apathy if they did so—with the sort of results sketched out by Walter Greenwood in his novel *Love on the Dole* (1933). Few women workers were organized in trade unions, and the numbers of 5 million trade unionists by even 1940 was still well below the figure of 6½ million for 1919 and 1920. The infrequency of labour disputes also reflected the subordinate role of trade unions at this time: 'In the years 1934−9 the number of working days lost as a result of disputes only once exceeded two million, whereas between 1919 and 1926 it had never been less than seven million and had averaged several times that figure.'[2]

Second, although many areas of the country which had depended on such traditional industries as coal, cotton, steel and ship-building did suffer severely in the depression—the North, Scotland and Wales—other regions actually expanded in the same decade, a contrast J.B.Priestley dwelt on in his *English Journey* of 1934. Motor cars, the electricity industry, advertising, chain stores, aircraft, housing, service industries like cinemas—these grew in the 1930s, but invariably they focused on the already relatively affluent Midlands and South. Likewise for those with a job the standard of living nudged upwards, and such institutions as building societies and hire purchase firms prospered.

Third, the Conservative Party remained a powerful and united body, in marked contrast to the Labour Party which 'lost' its leaders in 1931 and suffered from the trade unions' shortage of funds; later on, doubts about the Moscow trials weakened the Popular Front movement. Led in the first part of the period by the reassuring and avuncular figure of Stanley Baldwin, Conservative Party propaganda was also put over by means of the latest techniques:

a fleet of cinema vans scoured the country, speakers were trained in 'anti-socialist' arguments at the Party's residential colleages, and their campaigners were already immersed in the fledgeling social sciences and in American techniques of market research. And of course the 1931 election gave them a stranglehold on parliament which even the historian of the Conservative Party has described as 'an absurd and unhealthy situation, well calculated to muffle important issues and obscure the realities of the times'.[3]

But if the 1930s were in the main characterized by the strength of conservatism, a number of initiatives in retrospect can be seen to have laid the basis for the transformation of people's attitudes during the Second World War. Most notable was the Left Book Club which, founded in the summer of 1936, had nearly 60,000 members by 1938. The monthly *Left News* contained analyses both of the books themselves and the contemporary political situation, as well as keeping readers' groups in touch with each other. The Left Book Club introduced many people to active politics for the first time and provided a focus for everyone dissatisfied with the foreign policy of Neville Chamberlain, the prime minister from May 1937.

Other developments included *Picture Post*, set up in 1938, Penguin Specials from November 1937, Mass-Observation — a body which reported on 'the common people's' reaction to contemporary events — also dating from 1937, and a wave of publications in the second half of the 1930s which indicated the growing power of an influential social conscience; such books included Boyd Orr's *Food, Health and Income* (1936), M'Gonigle and Kirby's *Poverty and Public Health* (1936), the Pilgrim Trust's *Men Without Work* (1938), and Margery Spring Rice's *Working-class Wives* (1939). These works often included a depth of detail which Labour Party programmes, such as *For Socialism and Peace* (1934), conspicuously lacked. What was missing, however, was the popular support necessary to put pressure on the government of the day. This was to be remedied within the next few years.

Any summary of the 1930s in Britain must conclude, as John Saville has, that: 'the most striking political characteristic of the 1930s was the way in which successive Conservative governments were able to ignore, on all fundamental matters, the Labour Party inside Westminster and the political and industrial movements outside.[4] The tragedy was that this political failure led to such dire social and economic consequences for so many people.

Europe

In Europe during the 1920s and 1930s the major problem facing French and British diplomats concerned the handling of the Soviet Union. The February 1917 revolution had been welcomed by many liberals as the downfall of repressive czarism and the necessary prelude to the establishment of a parliamentary democracy. The October Revolution, bringing Lenin and the Bolsheviks to power, was something quite different and altogether more menacing, an attitude confirmed when the Soviet Union pulled out of the war and repudiated past debts.

The end of the First World War placed the diplomats on the horns of a dilemma. A vociferous public campaign demanded the hanging of the Kaiser and the payment of huge reparations by Germany; but there were fears that this might deliver the country over to Bolshevism or alternatively weaken her as a bulwark against the USSR. The dilemma for the Western powers of the relationship between Germany and the Soviet Union is one that underpins much of European history this century.

The solution adopted after the 1914 – 18 war was that of both forcing Germany to pay reparations of £6,600 million (which were not scheduled to finish until 1963) and of helping the counter-revolutionary White army in their attack on the Red forces of the Soviets. Winston Churchill was the driving force behind the decision to intervene against what he called 'the foul baboonery of Bolshevism', and in all British aid worth £100 million (much greater in today's prices) went to the Whites. To no avail, as their disorganized forces, composed of men heartily fed up with prolonged warfare, faded away, and public opposition in Britain to intervention was expressed by the 'hands off Russia' movement.

But if the new regime in the USSR could not be overthrown, then at least it might be surrounded by countries whose governments were reliably anti-Soviet. The Treaty of Locarno in 1925, for example, guaranteed Germany's western frontiers but, ominously for the future, carefully resisted the imposition of any barriers to possible expansion eastwards. A 'cordon sanitaire' of states in Central Europe necessitated support for such dictators as Horthy in Hungary and Pilsudski in Poland.

The economic depression of the 1930s, bringing widespread unemployment and dislocation, created the sort of conditions in which fascist demagogues could flourish. Mussolini had already seized power in Italy in 1922, and Hitler, immeasurably aided by the support he received from industrialists and bankers as well as the actions of the Communists who expended the major part of their energies attacking the Social Democrats and vice versa, was elected Chancellor in January 1933. King Boris maintained his despotic rule in Bulgaria, as did King Carol in Rumania, and they were joined by the dictatorships of King Alexander in Yugoslavia and of General Metaxas in Greece. Salazar came to power in Portugal in 1922 and outlawed all political parties other than his own.

Throughout central and eastern Europe the agricultural crisis of the 1930s exacerbated what was already an appalling situation springing from primitive farming techniques, overpopulation, lack of industrialization and general illiteracy. A cameo provided by Olivia Manning at the start of her *Balkan Trilogy*, describing conditions in Rumania just before the outbreak of the Second World War, typified the backwardness which was rife in interwar Europe.

This was the time of the evening promenade. Guy suggested they should walk a little way; but first, they had to pass through the purgatory of the hotel's attendant beggars. These were professional beggars, blinded or maimed by beggar parents in infancy. Guy, during his apprentice year, had grown accustomed, if not inured, to the sight of white eyeballs and running sores, to have stumps and withered arms and the breasts of nursing mothers thrust into his face. The Rumanians accepted all this as part of life and donated coins so small that a beggar might spend his day collecting the price of a meal.

Exploiting the general European instability it was not long

before the powers of Italy, Germany and Japan embarked upon programmes of military expansion. The League of Nations, a body set up in the aftermath of 'the war to end all war' in 1920, was intended to arbitrate on international disputes. But it lacked any machinery with which to enforce sanctions, economic or military, against those countries which transgressed its Covenant. More importantly, of the three major nations behind the League, America had retreated into splendid isolation, and Britain and France showed no inclination to enforce its provisions.

In September 1932 a Japanese army invaded Manchuria, setting up a puppet state which they called Manchuko. Chinese appeals to the League of Nations brought forth a commission which criticized Japan for its actions but did nothing more concrete, and when Japan left the League it was with Manchuko still intact. Leading politicans excused themselves on the grounds that Manchuria was a long way off and of no great interest to Europeans, but in 1934 there was another attempt — rather nearer home — by a major power to 'slim down' a weaker neighbour, when Italy invaded Abyssinia. This time the League imposed limited economic sanctions on Italy for its unprovoked aggression, but it soon became clear that only an oil embargo would be of consequence. This was never imposed, and the hypocrisy of British policy is illustrated by the fact that throughout the summer of 1935 Britain supplied arms to Italy whilst forbidding such exports to Abyssinia.[5] In May 1936, Emperor Haile Selassie fled the country and Mussolini was able to announce Abyssinia's annexation by Italy.

In July 1936 the Spanish Civil War began when Franco's rebel forces attacked the Republican government. The British and French governments immediately undertook to remain neutral and abide by the principle of non-intervention, as did the USSR. Hitler and Mussolini regarded this agreement with contempt and German troops arrived to assist Franco in November 1936. By March 1937, 80,000 Italians and 30,000 Germans were serving with the Nationalists. This superior military strength (Soviet assistance to the Republicans never matched that received by the Nationalists) slowly brought victory for Franco. The *Manchester Guardian* accurately referred to the Battle of Malaga in February 1937 as 'an Italian victory', and on 20 April 1937 German bombers destroyed the

Basque town of Guernica. The British and French governments averted their eyes from the fray; George Orwell wrote in *Homage to Catalonia* that 'the outcome of the Spanish war was settled in London, Paris, Rome, Berlin—at any rate not in Spain'. Neville Chamberlain, who had become prime minister in May 1937, recognized the existence of Franco's government in February 1939, although the civil war itself was still being fought until the end of March.

From the mid-1930s it was apparent that Italy and above all Nazi Germany were intent on executing a programme of military conquest. Still haunted by the spectre of Bolshevism—although the USSR had joined the League of Nations—the French and more especially the British governments adopted a policy of appeasement on the grounds that it was the lesser of two evils. Today this policy is usually presented as simply the naive aberration of one man, Neville Chamberlain. In fact appeasement was the product of a governing class's obsession with the threat of the Soviet Union.

Take, for example, Winston Churchill, who is invariably portrayed as spending the whole of the decade warning about the threat of Germany and Italy. This, however, is not what he was saying at the time. In May 1935 he described Mussolini as 'a really great man', and in October 1937 in the *News of the World* wrote of the 'amazing qualities of courage, comprehension, self-control and perseverance which he exemplifies'. In an article of 1935—which he republished in October 1937—Churchill referred to Hitler thus:

Although no subsequent political action can condone wrong deeds or remove the guilt of blood, history is replete with examples of men who have risen to power by employing stern, grim, wicked and even frightful methods, but who, nevertheless, when their life is revealed as a whole, have been regarded as great figures whose lives have enriched the story of mankind. So may it be with Hitler.[6]

Faced with such accommodating attitudes, and confirmed by the Anglo—German Naval Treaty of June 1935 which allowed both countries to maintain an equal number of submarines—a weapon that the Treaty of Versailles forbade Germany to possess—Hitler began to increase German influence in neighbouring countries. In July 1935 the Austrian Chancellor Dollfuss was murdered and the Austrian Nazi Party artificially built up. In March 1936 German troops marched into the Rhineland, an area stipulated by international agreement to be a demilitarized zone; the French government was prepared to take action, but the British held them back. And in March 1938 Austria was 'incorporated' into Germany; British reaction confined itself to Chamberlain's expression of his 'severest condemnation' in the House of Commons.

Chamberlain and other prominent people in Britain maintained that this was the only possible course of action. One veteran journalist, James Margach, has written about his experiences of Chamberlain's methods in the 1930s:

> Any question put across the table about, say, reports of the persecution of the Jews, Hitler's broken pledges or Mussolini's ambitions, would receive a response on well-established lines: he [Chamberlain] was surprised that such an experienced journalist was susceptible to Jewish-Communist propaganda.[7]

The newspaper proprietor Lord Beaverbrook forbade his *Daily Express* journalists from writing anything which might upset German ambassador von Ribbentrop, and Geoffrey Dawson, editor of the *Times*, censored his foreign correspondents' reports so as not to displease Hitler and the Nazis, often adding to their stories as well: 'I spend my nights dropping in little things which are intended to soothe them.' The politician and writer Harold Nicolson noted in his diary during 1938 that he had just met 'three young peers who state that they would prefer to see Hitler in London than a socialist administration.' Examples such as these can be quoted endlessly.[8]

Hitler next turned his attentions towards Czechoslovakia, presenting its government with a list of demands that amounted to a German takeover. Chamberlain flew to see Hitler and came back with the Munich settlement—an agreement which confirmed German domination of Czechoslovakia—announcing that 'I believe it is peace for our time'. The *Times* was in no doubt either, declaring that 'no conqueror returning from a victory on the battlefield had come adorned with nobler laurels'. In April 1939 Italy took the opportunity to occupy Albania. Chamberlain's only problem seemed to be that of running out of European countries with which to appease Hitler and Mussolini.

Today, the policy of appeasement is often justified on the grounds that, by playing for time, Britain was able to begin its rearmament programme. But was this really the case? Sir Thomas Inskip had been Minister of Defence since 1936, and in March 1939 he did indeed begin to supervise the building-up of Britain's military strength. 'Sir Thomas has put it on record that he got down on his knees on that March evening, 1939, and prayed for divine help in the work of rearming Britain. Next morning they gave him one room, one chair, and one secretary. He set to work.'[9]

Throughout these events the Soviet Union had been pressing for a policy of collective security against the designs of Hitler and Mussolini. The British government studiously ignored the Soviets over the Czech crisis, and the response to Soviet overtures throughout 1939 was half-hearted. A Foreign Office official was dispatched to Moscow in June 1939 and, in an atmosphere of accelerating crisis, the Anglo-French Military Mission took eleven days to prepare for its departure and then travelled by slow passenger boat to Leningrad — all of which contrasts with the hurried trips of Chamberlain himself to see Hitler by aeroplane. The end result was shattering: on 23 August 1939 the German and Soviet authorities announced that they had signed a non-aggression pact. The two countries which had always been thought of as diametrically opposed, fascism versus communism, were now joined together under the stimulus of nearly a decade of British and French equivocation and ambiguity. The pact itself, and the circumstances surrounding it, are almost a symbol of the catastrophies and betrayals so widespread throughout interwar Europe.

3. Britain during the war

In early September 1939 the Germans moved against Poland, a country allied to Britain. The Chamberlain government's ultimatum to Hitler expired on 3 September 1939 and Britain, together with France, declared war on Germany. This, the second major war to take place in Europe within 25 years, led to a conflict which provoked enormous political, social and economic changes within Britain: although less than half the number of troops died as had done in the First World War, the additional need to mobilize the civilian population ensured an approach subsequently termed 'total war'.

But this was some way in the future, and the British and French governments edged nervously into the fray. Article 1 of the Mutual Assistance Pact signed with Poland declared that in the event of an attack by a European power: 'The other Contracting Party will at once give the Contracting Party engaged in hostilities all the support and assistance in its power'. Between 2 and 20 September the German invaders smashed the Polish army, and under the secret protocol attached to the Nazi—Soviet pact Poland was partitioned between Germany and the Soviet Union. From now on Poland was to cease to exist.

What were the British and French governments doing to provide 'all the support and assistance in [their] power' whilst the German army swept all before them? How many guns, tanks and soldiers did they send to their beleaguered ally? The answer: none at all. Instead the British authorities confined their military operations to dropping millions of leaflets over Germany, urging the people to call upon their rulers to refrain from war-like activities. The folly of holding back from an attack on Germany in September

1939 was compounded by the knowledge that the German army had only 33 ill-equipped divisions available, as opposed to the French army's minimum of 80 divisions; and confirmed by the statements of all German chiefs of staff at the Nuremburg trials after the war, when they admitted that Germany would certainly have been defeated in 1939 if it had been forced to fight in the east against Poland and in the west against Britain and France.

The explanation for British policy, which the French tended to follow, lay in the government's lack of will to fight – as opposed merely to declare war on – Hitler's Germany. The hope remained that their policy of appeasement would finally satiate German territorial ambitions. In a speech at the House of Commons in October 1939, Chamberlain showed himself still prepared to bargain:

> Either the German government must give convincing proof of the sincerity of their desire for peace by definite acts and by provision of effective guarantees of their intention to fulfil their undertakings, or we must persevere in our duty to the end. It is for Germany to make her choice.

Touring France in December 1939 he remarked to an army commander (the future General Montgomery): 'I don't think the Germans have any intention of attacking us. Do you?'[1]

After the German success in Poland months passed when little seemed to be happening, and the war quickly became known as the 'phoney' or 'bore' war. The Nazis, utilizing to the full the resources of the Skoda armaments factories in Czechoslovakia and the iron ore of Poland, concentrated on building up their war offensive. The National government – Conservative in all but name – supposedly did the same, although the rate of progress appeared small. Umemployment remained at 1.5 million, no Ministry of Supply was created, the September budget scarcely introduced a war economy, prices spiralled upwards and the Ministy of Information reported widespread discontent with official apathy and complacency.

The government still comprised those men who had so enthusiastically approved the Munich settlement, save for the appointment of Winston Churchill to the Admiralty as a sop to the more belligerent Conservatives. Demands voiced in the House of Commons for bombing attacks on Nazi Germany embarrassed the government. When it was suggested to Kingsley Wood, the Minister of Air, that the Black Forest should be set on fire he replied: 'Are you aware it is private property? Why, you will be asking me to bomb Essen next'.

Others outside the government were worried about the implications of a war with Germany. For example, in January 1940 ten senior members of the House of Lords sent an explicit memorandum to the Prime Minister: 'It is now widely felt that, on a long view, the weakening or dismemberment of Germany would destroy the natural barrier against the western march of Bolshevism. We would suggest to you that this is a strong reason in favour of an early peace.'[2] Top-ranking ambassadors such as Sir Neville Henderson and Lord Lothian reiterated the same view.

Although the war had reached stalemate between Germany and the Anglo-French side, fighting had broken out elsewhere when the Soviet army launched a 'pre-emptive' strike on Finland in November 1939 in order to prevent that country's use as a launching pad for attacks on the USSR. Contrary to Stalin's forecasts, the Finnish forces put up a brave display, pinning down Russian troops in the frozen wastes and preventing a quick victory. The British and French governments, in marked contrast to their approach over Poland, assembled an army of 100,000 men who were all set to be sent into Finland when the Soviet side finally won in March 1940. The historian A.J.P.Taylor has written of this episode in his *English History 1914-15*:

The motives for the projected expedition to Finland defy rational analysis. For Great Britain and France to provoke war with Soviet Russia when already at war with Germany seems the product of a madhouse, and it is tempting to suggest a more sinister plan: switching the war on to an anti-Bolshevik course, so that the war against Germany could be forgotten or even ended.

British and French preparations in the west staggered on, secure in their confidence that the Maginot Line, in the throes of construction since 1930, would successfully repel attackers. The Foreign Office was even warned by various intelligence sources of the forthcoming German offensive against Belgium and France, but ignored it. General Ironside, chief of the Imperial General Staff, gave an interview to the *Daily Express* in April 1940: 'We would welcome a go at him [Hitler]. Frankly we would welcome an attack. We are sure of ourselves. We have no fears.' Chamberlain echoed this mood in April 1940 with his now infamous remark that 'Hitler has missed the bus'. This sense of complacency survived even the Norwegian campaign of April – May 1940 when Churchill initiated moves intended to cut off the German army from advantageous strategic positions. An ill-equipped British force was landed in Norway without skis and with only tourist maps to help them find their route; driven back by superior German troops, they had to be ignominiously evacuated. Military incompetence found itself trumped only by that of the Prime Minister himself, who succeeded in confusing the vital towns of Narvik and Larvik. Chamberlain's standing in the Gallup Polls – 57 per cent approval in March, 32 per cent in May – fell dramatically as public complaint at the blundering of the government increased. Desperately trying to stave off the growing pressure, Chamberlain attempted to broaden the basis of his administration by inviting the Labour Party to join him in office. This manoeuvre failed and Chamberlain finally resigned on 10 May 1940, to be replaced by Churchill.

On that same day the Germans attacked Holland and Belgium. Based on the ideas of blitzkrieg – rapid tank manoeuvres supported by aerial dive-bombing – the German forces quickly hurled back the French and British armies, which were led by men expecting another prolonged attritional war on the lines of 1914 – 18. The supposedly invincible Maginot Line counted for nothing as the German tanks simply outflanked it, advancing faster than the Allies could retreat, their communications in shreds and the French government frenziedly replacing elderly generals with elderly generals. At Dunkirk the way back was blocked by the Channel, which meant that the troops had to be shipped off the pier and beaches whilst under constant German fire, quite defenceless and out in the open.

Although the authorities made every effort to cover this up, it is clear that the troops' reaction as they reached Britain was one of anger and disgust at the extent to which German equipment and tactics were so far superior to their own. One book, *Guilty Men* by 'Cato' (of which Michael Foot was a co-author), was published in the summer of 1940, selling 250,000 copies and condemning 'the men of Munich' for the disastrous military situation. 'Here then in three words is the story. Flesh against steel. The flesh of heroes, but none the less, flesh. It is the story of an army doomed before they took the field'. Mass-Observation recorded the prevalent public attitude as being: 'This is not our war – this is a war of the high-up who use long words and have different feelings.' In other words Dunkirk was not, as it is assiduously represented today, a case of everyone pulling together in a patriotic explosion that transcended class differences, but rather a growing anger at the ineptitude of Britain's rulers both in the present and the past. Or, as the remark one diplomat kept hearing that summer put it: 'The British people will win the war in spite of the government.'

Guilty Men had also called for the prosecution of the war 'in total form', and the demands for 'total war' illustrated the realization both of the gravity of events now that Pétain's Vichy government had surrendered to the Germans, and of the requirements of modern warfare, which entailed the mobilization of the whole population in the war effort. Yet the implications of this were enormous. How could the majority of the population be mobilized into fighting to preserve the inequalities and injustices of the interwar years? Would the unemployed risk their lives to defend their right to be without a job, or the poor in order to live in squalid slums? If the 'common people' were making sacrifices to fight fascism, why should the wealthy and privileged escape the burdens? Was the reduced quantity of food and milk available to be distributed on the grounds of price, or that of need by means of rationing? Total war led to a much greater pooling of resources and the common sharing of dangers, and the authorities, slowly and with hesitation, had to come to terms with these changes.

For instance, food rationing was finally introduced in January 1940, although polls had shown that a large majority had been in favour of it ever since the outbreak of war – the *Daily Express* thundered away in vain at what it called 'that dreadful and terrible iniquity'. Excess Profits Tax, an attempt to restrict profiteering, had been levelled at a rate of 60 per cent since the September 1939 budget; that is, profiteering was acceptable if you were not too greedy. In May 1940 the rate of Excess Profits Tax was increased to 100 per cent. From July 1940 the government authorized the provision of free milk to mothers and young children, a measure which would have been derided by officials in the 1930s as wildly extravagant, and similarly the Board of Education directed that school meals should be available free to all. In a whole number of areas – evacuation and the blitzes, the campaigns for War Aims and postwar reconstruction, the alliance with the Soviet Union, the voracious interest of both civilians and troops in discussing and exploring social and political questions – the effects of the war had a democratizing and radicalizing tendency.

Evacuation had been introduced because the authorities thought air raids would follow immediately on the outbreak of war and they aimed to shift as many children as possible to safer country districts. Therefore on 1 September 1939 the task began of herding thousands of children to railway stations where they were packed off to their new homes, carrying small suitcases and with a label around their necks in case anyone should want to know who they were. This migration in the first three days of September saw a total of some 1.5 million people evacuated to different parts of the country.

The effect of evacuation lay in the revelations it brought of the want and degradation rife in slum and dockland Britain. As the *Economist* later expressed it in May 1943, evacuation was 'the most important subject in the social history of the war because it revealed to the whole people the black spots in its social life'.[3] Genteel middle-class households found their homes invaded by children who from habit crept under beds to go to sleep, or urinated over carpets, or who were crawling with vermin and possessed little more than the threadbare clothes which covered them. Platitudes shattered at this head-on collision with what government policies in the interwar years had really meant to the bulk of the population. A book published in 1943 by the Women's Group on Public Welfare, called *Our Towns*, has a first chapter entitled 'Evacuation: The Window through which Town Life was Seen', and Neville Chamberlain wrote in a private letter of September 1939: 'I never knew that such conditions existed, and I feel ashamed of having been so ignorant of my neighbours.'[4]

Others' reactions were harsher, such as the local dignitary who argued that Epping should not have to take any evacuees because 'I will not have these people billeted on our people.' The almost feudal atmosphere still prevalent in many villages saw the more affluent advancing compelling reasons, and doctors' certificates, as to why they should be 'spared'. Arthur Box-Bender, for example, the Conservative MP in Evelyn Waugh's *Sword of Honour* trilogy, has his country home declared a repository for 'national art treasures'. Neither was evacuation a problem for those with money, able to slip quietly away from the danger areas. The *Times* devoted an editorial in January 1941 to castigating those country hotels 'filled with well-to-do refugees, who too often have fled from nothing. They sit and read and knit and eat and drink and get no nearer the war than the news they read in the newspapers.'[5] Many of the evacuated children and pregnant mothers began to drift back to their homes when the bombs did not fall, one million having returned by January 1940. But the social effects of evacuation were more lasting, imprinting themselves firmly on a middle-class consciousness which had thought 'the condition of England' question safely confined to the 1840s.

Throughout the summer of 1940 the Battle of Britain was being fought, with Goering and his Luftwaffe striving to clear the skies of British planes as a necessary prelude to a German invasion. By September 1940 it was apparent that the bravery and hard work of the RAF technicians and pilots, coupled with the benefits of radar, had thwarted German plans; instead their tactics switched to bombarding towns and cities in the hope of destroying morale and essential factories. 'The Blitz' on London began in the afternoon of 7 September 1940, with the capital bombed for the next 57 consecutive nights. Other provincial cities such as Glasgow, Southampton, Manchester, Plymouth and Birmingham also suffered heavy raids, and as a result the political and social consequences of the German bombing were felt in most urban centres throughout the country.

One of the most immediate changes following a raid was that

the bombing had the effect of bringing people closer together, neighbours who had not spoken to each other in twenty years sharing cups of tea and recounting their 'bomb stories'. Clearly everyone was in it together; the raids were experienced collectively and with a relative levelling of class barriers, breaking down old inhibitions and restraints, militating against the fragmenting tendencies of peacetime life. Some of the shelters developed into communal centres as people grouped together in places where they thought they would be safe from the bombs. The authorities had decided that underground stations were not to be used as refuges because of their fear of 'deep-shelter mentality' — shelterers not wishing to emerge after the raids had finished. This order was simply disregarded as inner-city dwellers bought ordinary tube tickets and then took up their places on the platforms.

At first the sanitation left a certain amount to be desired, but slowly spontaneous forms of organization sprang up initiating a whole range of activities in which all participated. There were singsongs and concerts, performances of plays, libraries and magazines, darts leagues, gramophone concerts, variety programmes and so on. The East End shelters in particular developed a 'little republic' atmosphere — some of them contained more than 10,000 occupants — as they elected delegates and shelter marshals, painted murals on the walls and organized their own 'Blitz dive' canteens and health clinics. Generally, as one observer, Ritchie Calder, wrote at the time, 'the inarticulate become convincingly articulate', primarily because people's creativity and resources, usually wasted or ignored, found an outlet and expression in this collective effort.[6]

However, these images of endurance and stoicism — the newspapers were heavily censored, often quite willingly, to ensure the maintenance of the 'Britain can take it' picture — should not mask the tensions and hostilities which the German bombs also caused. Some shelters differed markedly from others: the one at the Savoy Hotel had a restaurant, cabaret and dormitory. Not all homeless East Enders found their West End hosts friendly.

For example, a rich family in Belgravia with a large house, had a bombed out family from Whitechapel billeted

on them. The rich put the poor in the servants'
quarters—that is to say, under the eaves and nearest to the
bombers—and refused to let them shelter in the basement
where they themselves slept.[7]

A few local authorities broke down completely under the
pressure, and others tried to insist upon a 'poor law' approach
to those bombed out, with rest centres for the victims originally
intended to provide bully-beef sandwiches rather than hot meals.
The Treasury had claimed that mobile canteens were grossly ex-
pensive, and so in response local groups of people set up commercial feeding centres on their own initiative, finally pressuriz-
ing the Ministry of Food into establishing 'British Restaurants'
where cheap hot food was served at all times of the day or night.
In addition, the Assistance Board, which was responsible for all
bomb victims, gradually changed from a stance whereby assistance
was doled out grudgingly and only if recipients acknowledged their
inferiority, to the attitude that help should be provided solely on
the basis of human need. This of course was the sole criterion
used by the newly-created Emergency Medical Service, established
because the 1930s patchwork of private and health insurance
schemes was found to be totally inadequate.

All over the country the blitzes occasioned countless examples
of men and women hazarding their lives for others, not just the
firefighters, the ARP (Air Raid Precaution) wardens, police, doctors
and nurses but also many others not in uniform whose actions provided a permanent rebuke to those cynical about 'human nature'.

In June 1941 the Germans invaded the Soviet Union, and,
like Napoleon and Gustavus Adolphus before, Hitler and his troops
soon discovered the perils of such a course of action. In Britain
there was an upsurge of enthusiasm for the new Soviet ally,
strengthened by news of the self-destructive 'scorched earth' tactics
adopted by the Red army which entailed the blowing up of anything
that might be of use to the advancing German army. Finally, at
the end of 1942, the Red army confronted the Germans at Stalingrad and fought out a long and bloody battle which ended in
January 1943 with the surrender of General Paulus and 90,000
of his soldiers. After Stalingrad it was virtually certain that the

Germans would be defeated, in large part due to the Soviet Union which had had hundreds of cities and towns devastated and was to lose 20 million people in the process.

At the time of the Nazi—Soviet pact in 1939 few people in Britain outside the Communist Party had a good word to say about the Soviet Union—after 1941 few had a bad word to say. 'Aid to Russia weeks', 'Red army days', celebrations of the 25th anniversary of the Revolution, Stalingrad festivals, all were organized throughout the country as people strove to express their gratitude to their new ally. Conservative MPs and councillors found no incongruity in standing up to sing 'The Internationale' at the end of such festivals, and Mrs Churchill headed the Aid to Russia fund, which finally amassed £8 million. King George VI presented a specially made Sword of Stalingrad to that city, although not before it had attracted huge crowds as it was exhibited around Britain. The works of Lenin and Stalin were even recommended by educational authorities for school study! Books like Sidney and Beatrice Webb's *Soviet Communism—A New Civilization* and Dean Hewlett Johnson's *The Socialist Sixth of the World* notched up huge sales, the latter selling over a million copies in the United States.

As Mary Stocks, the historian of the Worker's Educational Association, has written of the army camps during the war: 'everywhere men wanted to know about Russia—the new ally whose dogged resistance has caused a spectacular diversion of German war potential and brought respite to our bombed cities.'[8] The membership of the Communist Party rose to over 60,000 and the *Daily Worker*, freed from the ban imposed on it in January 1941, was being read by at least four times that number. A well-organized and powerful 'Second Front' campaign (the 'first' front was that between the German and the Soviet armies) maintained pressure on the coalition government to begin military operations in Europe and so provide some relief for the Russians.

The shaking up and dislocation of traditional beliefs and values stimulated a ferment of discussion, and all over the country there developed an overwhelming enthusiasm for knowledge about politics and contemporary affairs, reading and theatre, music, poetry and education. Organizations and bodies staggering along in the 1930s suddenly found their membership rising dramatically, supplemented by the formation of new groups which sprang up everywhere. All of them played a part in the making of a thriving and stimulating political culture in Britain.

Both the Workers' Educational Association and the National Council of Labour Colleges reported their membership and classes boosted despite the disruption caused by mobilization and the bombing. The Socialist Medical Association, for example, the organization campaigning for a free national health service, saw their numbers and active branches quadruple.[9] Civilians were eager to argue about new ideas well into the evening despite a long day at work. The National Fire Service instituted discussion schemes, as did the Industrial Discussion Clubs from 1943 and, for instance, groups in Bristol spent six months of 1944 debating the need for a national health service. The 'Brains Trust', a radio programme established in 1941 on which a panel of experts answered listeners' questions, soon secured an audience of ten million, inspiring scores of invitations throughout Britain organized on more democratic lines and which directly addressed political topics.

The sense of participation was also exemplified by the saga of the Home Guard or 'Dad's army'. A broadcast by Anthony Eden, Secretary of State for War, in May 1940 calling for a civilian defence force provoked 250,000 men to give their names within 24 hours; by the end of June nearly 1.5 million had enrolled. Although military ranks and the use of commissioned officers were later introduced, the Home Guard did operate as a rather more democratic civilian force than the stiffly hierarchical regular army. George Orwell described it as 'a people's army officered by Blimps'.[10]

The thirst for discussion and debate was also very apparent within the armed forces themselves. War Office surveys in the first half of 1941 revealed that the morale of the forces generally was very low, this fact being attributed to the troops' suspicion of the military leaders and their enthusiasm for engaging in this anti-fascist war. It was also reported that political discussion was widespread, and the Army Bureau of Current Affairs (ABCA) was founded in June 1941 both to channel these discussions and to keep amused all those men now based in Britain. However, such a mood was not one that could easily be contained and the publications issued, like *Current Affairs*, *The British Way and Purpose* booklets, and the *Why We Fight* series, reflected the radical shifts taking place; in particular they focused on the kind of Britain that should be built after the war, tackling such topics as the need for a levelling of incomes or a comprehensive system of social security. Later in the war the growing self-confidence of the troops was demonstrated by their creation of 'forces parliaments' – in effect, rank-and-file debating societies – which enquired into the merits of such measures as the nationalization of the banks, the most famous being that held at Cairo from November 1943 to April 1944.

This abiding interest in contemporary affairs was fuelled and sustained by a wave of radical journalism and criticism as publishers found, for possibly the only time ever in this country, that left-wing material was assured of a large readership. For instance, a typical Penguin Special of 1940 such as Harold Laski's *Where Do We Go From Here?* rapidly sold 80,000 copies, and writers like Ritchie Calder, Tom Wintringham, George Orwell, Michael Foot, James Cameron, Fyfe Robertson, G.D.H. and Margaret Cole, even churchpeople like William Temple, using vivid and accessible language that appealed to a popular and not just a specialist audience, were widely read. Many then enterprising and iconoclastic publications provided a wide variety of forums – the *Daily Mirror*, the *Evening Standard*, the *Daily Herald*, the *Sunday Pictorial* and the *News Chronicle*, the *New Statesman* and *Picture Post* – as did *Tribune*, especially when Aneurin Bevan became its editor from late 1941.

Another area in which wartime conditions transformed conventional approaches was that of culture, of books and theatre, music and art. The outbreak of war had badly hit the entertainment industry, first with the blackout and then the German air raids – in London during the first years only two theatres, the Windmill and Unity, remained open – and much of the population was dispersed into entirely new districts and places of work, locations totally unsuitable for the traditional arts routines: war hostels, factory canteens, Nissen huts, gun sites, bomb shelters, rest centres. Organizations had to respond to these new circumstances, and in doing so they ventured before vast new audiences and demonstrated the tremendous vitality and enthusiasm left untapped by the commercial system.

The Council for the Encouragement of Music and the Arts (CEMA) was founded in 1939 with the tasks of employing out of work artists and organizing musical activities for evacuation centres. This developed into the system of 'music travellers', who roamed the country playing before people in places far removed from the concert hall, and CEMA then expanded into the field of theatre. It funded the Old Vic, led by Sybil Thorndike and Lewis Casson, when they were evacuated from London and toured South Wales and County Durham, setting up their base in Burnley; and from October 1942 CEMA instituted its own theatrical circuit by establishing 14 touring companies, as well as funding such initiatives as the performance of ballet and opera in the parks of cities like London and Nottingham. By 1943, for instance, CEMA was giving over 4,500 factory concerts a year, sometimes before audiences of up to 7,000.[11]

The problems for the commercial stage during the war enabled a number of experimental theatre projects to come to the fore. The ABCA Play Unit developed out of the various army education schemes and sought ways of dramatizing current events with plays like *Where Do We Go From Here?* and *Lease-Lend*. The unit performed at gun sites and in Nissen huts, and therefore had to introduce a form of theatre that dispensed with the old traditional proscenium barrier approach which rigidly separated the performers from the audience. Instead a documentary style was evolved which kept scenery to a minimum and made use of bold lighting effects, together with the use of speakers from the hall and action amongst the audience, concentrating wholly on the esentials of the plays and ignoring the usual 'production values' of the West End stage. Unity Theatre in London formed a mobile unit that played to the audiences at tube shelters, putting on both the classics and a variety programme. Similar Unity theatres were formed all over the country, for example in Glasgow in 1941, and eventually a national federation was set up. Joan Littlewood's Theatre Workshop remained active, the Co-op formed a People's Entertainment Society in 1942, and amongst amateurs the British

Drama League reached its highest-ever membership in 1944.[12]

The war years also witnessed a tremendous upsurge in the demand for books, assisted by the popular outcry which beat off attempts to impose a purchase tax — expenditure on books rose from £9 million in 1939 to £23 million in 1945. The expansion of the book industry did not mean an increased regurgitation of 'escapist' publications. The range and subject matter of the books illustrated a consuming interest in contemporary affairs — for example from 1943 there was a wave of books dealing with planning and reconstruction. Paperbacks, introduced by Allen Lane in 1935, were extremely popular and the sales of poetry books numbered not their usual hundreds but thousands.

CEMA and ENSA (Entertainments National Service Association, also known as Every Night Something Awful), Basil Dean's organization for the troops, were primarily responsible for music during the war with ENSA providing over two-and-a-half million performances for servicemen and factory workers. The London Philharmonic Orchestra which in the 1930s had been a fairly orthodox London-based concern, was transformed during the war into Musical Culture Ltd. Its base was a decrepit old music hall in Golders Green and it concentrated on taking the works of composers like Beethoven and Mozart to entirely new audiences in unusual settings, stimulating enormous enthusiasm. The War Artists Advisory Committee was established to document and record life on the 'home front', and artists such as Henry Moore, Graham Sutherland and Stanley Spencer produced some of their best work under these conditions. Similarly some striking posters and cartoons were used, and the documentary style was also evident in the works of the Crown Film Unit, like Harry Watt's *Target for Tonight* and Humphrey Jennings's *Fires were Started*.

The above are only a small sample of the multitude of cultural activities that flourished during the war, an expression of some of the creative impulses unleashed. The monthly journal *Our Time* detailed all these events, describing the developments as the birth of 'a people's culture'.

All too aware of the spurious 'homes fit for heroes' promises after the last war, the interest in plans for postwar reconstruction was both more thoughtful and specific. *Picture Post* published 'A

Plan for Britain' in January 1941 which emphasized the need for a just postwar Britain and received sacks of letters from readers all over the world, and a torrent of books and periodicals were issued tackling the same subject.[13] However it was the Beveridge Report, published in December 1942, which became the focus of much optimism.

Sir William Beveridge was a former civil servant, a supporter of the Liberal Party, and now the head of an Oxford college, who had been asked by the coalition government to draw up some proposals regarding peacetime economic and social programmes. The Ministry of Information had continually referred to the building up of the public's postwar expectations, and the Beveridge Report — *Report on Social Insurance and Allied Services* — chimed in perfectly with this mood, selling well over 600,000 copies.

The Report was grounded on the assumptions that any government after the war would introduce family allowances, a comprehensive health system and the maintenance of full employment — clearly a far cry from the 1930s. Broadcasts by Beveridge underlined the change in attitudes induced by the war:

> The security plan in my report is a plan for securing that no-one in Britain willing to work while he can is without income sufficient to meet at all times the essential needs of himself and his family. The security plan is only a means of redistributing national income so as to put first things first, so as to ensure abolition of want before the enjoyment of comfort.

Further, Beveridge suggested that his scheme should be introduced on 1 July 1944.

Opinion polls immediately showed that nearly nine out of every ten people welcomed the Report and thought it should be implemented without delay, a reaction confirmed when Churchill and the coalition government attempted to play down enthusiasm for the Report. A Social Security League sprang up to campaign for 'Beveridge in full' and public enthusiasm mirrored the inexorable swing to the left taking place throughout the war. Gallup Polls published in the *News Chronicle* from 1942 substantiated this impression, as did the soundings taken by Mass-Observation. In mid-1943, for instance, they found that 25 per cent of a sample estimated the war had moved their political opinions to the left, and only 4 per cent to the right.

One obstacle in the way of the expression of these changes was the electoral truce agreed by the three major parties; none of them would contest the others' seats as they became vacant through death or resignation. This pact, although nearly overturned by delegates at the 1942 Labour Party Conference, ensured that independent candidates would have to fight against the combined party machines of Conservative, Liberal and Labour. Some still managed to do it, like the journalist Tom Driberg at Maldon in June 1942, but the major impetus came with the founding of the 'Common Wealth' party in July 1942.

Reflecting general frustration at the slow leisurely pace of organized politics, Common Wealth injected its own brand of ethical socialism. Again echoing wartime popular radicalism, its programme called for 'common ownership of the great productive resources with democracy in industry as well as in politics', and the party approved of the principles behind the Beveridge Report. By 1944 Common Wealth claimed to have 400 branches all over the country and 15,000 members, and it now had two MPs to its name.

But although there was quite clearly a radical transformation and shaking up of people's attitudes and views throughout Britain in the Second World War, it would be wrong to exaggerate these changes. Many of the shifts described were only in fact superficial, and the rest of this chapter will focus on some of the weaknesses and continuities. However, to do this is not in any way to denigrate the generosity and optimism of a great deal of the popular mood during the war.

The tremors sent through the British establishment in 1940 by the effects of evacuation, Dunkirk and the Blitz did not in the end bring about the collapse of traditional institutions — unlike in Europe, where they forcibly disintegrated due to the Nazi occupation. For instance Chamberlain was replaced not by some fiery radical but by the scrupulously constitutional Winston Churchill, the man who had so ardently championed both the cause of the

Empire and an aggressive government stance during the General Strike of 1926. Churchill further emphasized this when, in October 1940, he accepted the leadership of the Conservative Party; and similarly the leaderships of the Labour Party and the trade unions found their positions being shored up in the early anxious years of the war as they successfully called upon their members to 'rally round!'

Throughout the war Churchill's main preoccupation was that of international affairs and questions of domestic policy were left largely to the other members of his coalition government. By October 1942 three leading figures in the Labour Party — Attlee, Bevin and Morrison — were members of the seven-man war cabinet and Ernest Bevin in particular, as Minister of Labour, was in a key position to influence the government's social and economic programmes. A number of other Labour ministers were also well-placed lower down in the government echelons.

On the other hand the Labour Party was now an integral part of the coalition administration, unable to offer radical alternatives that would in any way jeopardize the 'national unity' to which they were committed. The Labour members of the cabinet seemed to adapt quite straightforwardly to their colleagues' conservatism. Attlee remarked later that Churchill's antipathy towards socialism pervaded their meetings, but he adds that this never led to divisions along party lines; and Richard Casey, an Australian diplomat allowed to attend some meetings of the cabinet, supports this in his memoirs when he writes: 'practically all the Labour Ministers integrate loyally and helpfully with the Tories, particularly Bevin.'[14]

As the leader of the country's biggest trade union, the Transport and General Workers' Union, Bevin was also ideally placed to further his movement's contacts with government and employers. The hope behind the integrationist policy of Bevin and Citrine was that the government would have to acquiesce in certain demands of the unions. The other side of the coin was that the trade union movement would have to give a bit too. As Keith Middlemas has written in his *Politics in Industrial Society*:

The emergency of 1940 led to a ban on strikes and

lockouts which lasted until 1951, the submission of trade
disputes to compulsory arbitration, stringent penalties
against unofficial strikes, and limitations on industrial
freedom of speech – things never achieved by the most ex-
treme advocates of coercion in 1916 – 18. Yet these powers
were taken, not in the manner of Hindenburg and Luden-
dorff, nor as a result of any electoral mandate, but after
the consent of the trade union movement, represented by
2,000 executive delegates at the Central Hall,
Westminister, had been given to their representative, the
Minister of Labour, on 25 May 1940.[15]

Certainly the war did bring gains for many working people
and their families. There was full employment, wages rose substantially faster than prices, rationing ensured that essential food and
goods would reach everyone, trade union membership rose from
just over 6 million to 8 million, the incidence of infant mortality
and tuberculosis dropped. But the tripartitism between state,
employers and employees restricted the demands of organized
labour and often, as with Churchill's steadfast refusal to repeal
the Trade Disputes Act 1927 as a gesture of 'national unity', there
was little that could be done to achieve their demands.

Techniques of modern labour planning flourished in such an
atmosphere, a combination of the stick and the carrot. The stick
comprised Order 1305, passed in 1940, declaring strikes illegal;
the Essential Work Order of 1941 which required skilled workers
to register and meant they could be directed to enter employment
in the 'essential category'; and Regulation 1AA which gave the
authorities power to prosecute those who called for strikes. The
carrot was made up of a series of bodies working with the
employers to boost production such as the Production Councils,
the Joint Consultative Committees and Joint Production Committees. All these devices tended to strengthen the state's embrace
of the trade union leadership and to weaken the pressure exerted
by the rank and file – the TUC was working within organized industry rather than restructuring it. By 1944 it was clear that the
TUC realized the future might demand of them a more explicit
role in restraining their members; in their *Post-War*

Reconstruction: Interim Report they argued:

> In the circumstances in which the threat of the 'sack' no
> longer operates in industry (that is, in conditions of full
> employment), a system of self-discipline which is approved
> by the workers and undertaken by their collective organiza-
> tion will be required.

Appeals to patriotism and loyalty did not, however, totally
carry the day, as the number of unofficial strikes during the war
testifies, showing an increase when compared with the 1930s
figures. In a repeat of events in the First World War, shop stewards'
committees emerged to fill in the gap between the trade union
leadership and the shop floor opened up by the former's incor-
poration into the machinery of government. But, above all, in a
period when many men and women began to think seriously for
the first time about politics and question the priorities of the society
in which they lived, both the Labour Party and the trade unions
acted as a brake on this movement. One engineer, J.T.Murphy,
working in an aircraft factory in 1941, recorded that the workforce
were disappointed with the Labour Party leaders as being 'the office
boys of the government', a criticism echoed by Mass-Observation
studies throughout the war which found widespread disillusion with
the leaders of the labour movement; for example *The Journey
Home*, published by Mass-Observation in 1944, documented the
persistent complaints about the lack of 'forward leadership'
displayed by them.[16]

The tight censorship system in use throughout the war attempted
to restrain the more radical expression of changing moods. The
BBC's rigorous approach—they even set up an 'anti-slush committee' designed to exclude 'psychologically unreliable' popular
songs from the air—often seemed to slip from justifiably not giving
any information to the Germans towards the castration of explicitly
political material. Harold Nicolson gave a broadcast just after the
Dunkirk evacuation which accusingly pointed the finger at British
and French politicians for the fiasco. It resulted in him being
discreetly taken off the BBC. J.B.Priestley found his second series
of *Postscripts* talks stopped, as he recounts in his autobiography,
Margin Released:

When I was brought back, after much clamour, I added some minutes and more edge to my talks. This time I was taken off the air... I received two letters and one was from the Ministry of Information, telling me that the BBC was responsible for the decision to take me off the air, and the other was from the BBC saying that a directive had come from the Ministry of Information to end my broadcasts. While blaming each other, I think both of them were concealing the essential fact—that the order to shut me up had come from elsewhere.

The Brains Trust, with its audience of up to 11 million, had to conform to strict regulations which stipulated that controversial issues—such as equal pay for men and women—should be avoided. Nor did the BBC merely censor news but sometimes also played a more active part in actually making it up. For example de Gaulle was built up as a politican in order to combat the feared strength of the Communist Party in postwar France, and the Foreign Office 'asked' the BBC to omit from their news broadcasts any mention of the exploits of Tito's partisans in Yugoslavia; instead the praise was to be heaped on General Mihailovic's right-wing Chetniks.

Newspapers had to be submitted to the scrutiny of a censorship committee headed by an Admiral Thomson. Again the point at issue is not so much that of preventing the careless giving of information to the Nazis, but the way in which the censorship expanded to cover matters politically sensitive to the government. The Home Secretary, Herbert Morrison, closed down the *Daily Worker* for 18 months from January 1941 when the Communist Party was arguing for a negotiated settlement with Germany. The *Daily Mirror* and *Sunday Pictorial* were continually threatened with closure, not for opposing the war but because, in Churchill's words, they were exploiting 'those grievances which lead to class dissension' and for 'persistent attacks on officers holding high ranking appointments'. The *Daily Mirror's* criticism of such targets was clearly in tune with public feeling—its circulation jumped from less than 2 million in 1939 to 3 million by 1946. Ministers kept up the pressure on the paper's proprietors for some months, and in March 1942 they were severely warned about the future content of their papers, although Churchill had wanted the *Daily Mirror* suppressed there and then. But if it was thought unadvisable to ban national dailies, then at least the government could suddenly post particularly irritating journalists out of the country, as Bill Connor ('Cassandra' of the *Daily Mirror*) and Frank Owen found out. *Picture Post* was another publication that fell foul of 'the blue pencil'.

The War Office kept a watchful eye on the selection and content of subjects to be discussed by the troops. Conservative MPs insisted that the Army Bureau of Current Affairs was indoctrinating the troops, but what they ignored was the general context in which such discussions took place — the radical temper made this inevitable. Certain lecturers were proscribed by the War Office, and in January 1943 the ABCA summary of the Beveridge Report was withdrawn without any explanation and replaced six months later by an exceptionally vapid document. Most notoriously of all, the military authorities forcibly terminated the Cairo forces' parliament in April 1944 after it had voted overwhelmingly to nationalize the banks. War correspondents were forbidden from sending home stories about the parliament; all mail from Egypt to Britain was censored, and the War Office attempted to send the 'ringleaders' to remote outposts around the globe. What the authorities simply could not come to terms with was the fact that the various forces' parliaments were not isolated and treasonable incidents provoked by atypical agitators, but spontaneous expressions of the political changes occurring amongst British troops everywhere.

Much of the journalism and writings of the war years undoubtedly helped raise the level of political culture in Britain, but often the approach and language used was rather naive. Many bitter attacks were launched at the 'old gang' or 'the men of Munich', yet they tended to personalize such issues into a loathing of Chamberlain himself. The rhetoric employed sometimes degenerated into extolling the virtues of some mythical and essentially decent England, ignoring any deeper structural analysis of British society. Ritchie Calder ended his first book on the Blitz with the rather vague exhortation: 'We must harness this new dynamic energy to the constructive purposes of peace, to the regeneration of the world... In peace, as in war, let us say: "CARRY ON LONDON".'[17] Similarly J.B.Priestley's collections *Postscripts* and *Out of the People* seemed to suggest that if people willed it hard enough then all the old inequalities would simply disappear and everyone would live happily ever after.

The largely enthusiastic response to the Beveridge Report also reflected some superficialities and limitations. The Report did not advocate a system whereby the onus was on society to provide 'work or full maintenance'. Instead, employees were to provide through individual contributions some of what they might or might not receive in benefits. The attitudes towards women expressed throughout the Report indicated the grip of assumptions concerning female dependency on the husband, and in particular their duty to reverse the falling birthrate: 'In the next 30 years housewives as mothers have vital work to do in ensuring the adequate continuance of the British race and of British ideals in the world.' George Orwell wrote of the Report that

> people seem to feel that this very moderate measure of reform is almost too good to be true. Except for the tiny interested minority, everyone is pro-Beveridge – including left-wing newspapers which a few years ago would have denounced such a scheme as semi-fascist – and at the same time no-one believes that Beveridge's plan will actually be adopted.

Aneurin Bevan reminded readers of *Tribune* that the Beveridge Report was not the product of a socialist, but that of an 'honest Liberal'.[18]

Symptomatic of this woolliness was the frequency with which the label 'revolution' was bandied around in order to describe the political and economic changes occurring in Britain. Hamilton Fyfe published a book entitled *Britain's Wartime Revolution*, and even the left-wing academic Harold Laski issued his *Reflections on the Revolution of Our Time* in which he developed the notion of 'revolution by consent'. Clearly some of the changes since 1939 had been pretty drastic – at least compared with the 1930s – but by no stretch of the imagination was it a 'revolution' when British institutions like the monarchy and the Civil Service remained quite intact.

Common Wealth was another group which eschewed specifics in favour of well-intentioned generalities – their principles of 'common ownership', 'vital democracy' and 'morality in politics' could, and did, mean all things to all people. Sir Richard Acland, the party's guiding light, was a former Liberal and his policies often seemed vague: 'the passion which alone can carry us through to victory is more than the hunger of an oppressed class for improved conditions. It must be a moral, even a religious passion for right human relations.' Similarly their relationship with the Labour Party remained ambiguous: were they trying to revitalize or to replace it? No one was quite sure.[19]

That left just one other party in Britain which might have seized the chance of channelling and leading the popular groundswell, the Communist Party. In January 1941 the Party organized a 'people's convention' which registered widespread discontent with the handling of the war. After the German invasion of the Soviet Union in June of that year the 'imperialist war' changed overnight into a 'people's war'. Consequently the Party campaigned to boost war production and minimize strikes or shop-floor indolence in order to aid 'our gallant Soviet ally'. The National Shop Stewards Committee, revived in 1940 to ensure that trade union rights and privileges were not extinguished during the war, found itself unable to decide whether trade unionists' rights should in fact be ignored if this led to increased production. The electoral truce was to be upheld so as not to disturb the Churchill government; and thus the bizarre situation arose at Wallasey in April 1942 that the Communist Party supported the Conservative candidate against the left-wing independent, who refused to recognize the truce.

The Communist Party's analysis of contemporary issues from 1941 onwards was therefore couched in the most simplistic and nationalist terms. Did or did not this proposed course of action stimulate the war effort? Membership increased rapidly as it was bound to do, but the Ministry of Information carefully arranged that 'Aid for Russia' weeks and so on were fronted by Conservatives and Liberals, reducing the amount of political mileage to be extracted from them by the left. In any case, as Mass-Observation found, 'ordinary people put British communism in a watertight compartment away from communism in Russia which is Russian, and ''different'' '. J.T.Murphy discovered in his air-craft factory that people were conscious of the Communist Party's previous 'imperialist war' propaganda and as a result suspicious of their new-found enthusiasm for the war. The Communist Party was as a result unable to provide any sustained 'forward leader-ship' or alternatives during the war.[20]

The limitations of the mood of wartime popular radicalism were those of any movement which lacks conscious political leader-ship and a coherent analysis or programme for action. The strengths of this mood meant that, for example, Churchill was prevented from quietly burying the Beveridge Report as he had wished. The weaknesses meant the inability to formulate a more far-reaching alternative to Beveridge which incorporated but went beyond his proposals; nor to counter the growing acceptance of the ideas of J.M.Keynes, whose tentative suggestions of the 1930s were to become the orthodoxy of the 1940s and later.

This meant that much of the detail in the blueprints for postwar reconstruction were in fact drawn up by government committees themselves with their succession of white papers. The political and social consciousness of the majority of the population in Britain was at a higher level by 1945 than before or since. But this nebulous mood never really translated into effective and sustained action—and when, in the second half of the 1940s, this mood came under intense pressure from a number of forces, it withered away.

4. The war in Europe

The German army, defeated in the First World War, had been spurred on by its failures into revolutionizing conventional thinking about military tactics and strategy. In particular, German theorists developed an approach very different from the 1914–18 war's emphasis on slow attritional pressure supported by heavy bombardment; instead mobility was to be of paramount importance, with fast-moving tanks and armoured vehicles, supported by aerial attack, surprising the enemy and rapidly pushing home their advantage. This concept, known as 'blitzkrieg', was in marked contrast to the ideas of the British and French General Staffs who remained fixated on the last war with its mud and trenches. Those men who did recognize the changes brought about by the tank, such as Captains de Gaulle and Liddell Hart, were disregarded, unlike Guderian in Germany, whose innovations were enthusiastically received by Hitler.

By the end of the 1930s the Germans had steadily expanded their armed forces, drawing upon their experience fighting for Franco's Nationalists to correct mistakes and patch up defects. The Nazis had also shrewdly built up native fascist parties in the countries they planned to annex—in Austria under Seyss-Inquart and in Czechoslovakia under Heinlein—and in other countries there were fascist sympathizers in prominent positions; that is where they were not, as in many Balkan and Mediterranean states, already in power.

Throughout the winter of 1939–40 the Germans re-equipped their forces, with the Allies following suit at a much slower rate. The 'phoney war' further sapped Allied morale, and when Hitler launched the spring offensive of 1940 his army was better led, technically superior and, just as important, faced by troops whose commanders, politicians and rulers lacked the political will to fight back with any determination. Appeasement had been no misguided policy of a few naive individuals but something that had deeply infected the leaders of many countries, and it was impossible for them to reverse their attitudes overnight.

And, literally, it would have needed to have been overnight as the German army swept all before it: Denmark capitulated without a struggle in April 1940; Holland surrendered on 15 May and Belgium on 28 May; Norway was under German control by 10 June and, on 14 June, Paris was occupied, again without resistance. On 22 June the Armistice between France and Germany was drawn up, partitioning France into an occupied and an unoccupied zone—the latter the Vichy regime under Marshal Pétain. The Italians entered the war that same month, and by the end of the year Germany had concluded treaties with the governments of Hungary and Rumania; the annexations of Bulgaria, Greece and Yugoslavia were inevitable and only a matter of months away. The fascist regimes of Spain and Portugal remained on the sidelines. A measure of the lack of military resistance encountered by the Germans is that they lost little more than 25,000 men in occupying most of the continent.

In other words, by the end of 1940 the whole of Europe was under fascist domination, barring only Britain and the Soviet Union which, still observing the non-aggression pact with Germany, had spent the intervening months occupying Finland and large tracts of Poland on the grounds that such territories were vital for their defence. Millions of people were now under the sway of an ideology which glorified a supposed 'master race', destroying political parties and trade unions, exterminating Jews and Slavs as sub-human species, and adopting a barbarism which treated the inhabitants of occupied countries as less than animals.

And yet, out of this terrible crucible of 1940, slowly, painfully, emerged a genuine stirring throughout much of the world determined to shed this fascist yoke. Sometimes the mood was primarily negative in the sense of being anti-fascist and little else; but more often the groundswell contained positive demands and achievements which looked beyond the end of the conflict, towards the construction of a postwar world in which fascism, poverty and mass unemployment, all so prevalent in the 1930s, would be extinct and out of place.

At first, throughout 1940 and much of 1941, occupied Europe was quiescent, clearly in a state of shock. Everything seemed dislocated and confused: in France alone there were six million refugees on the roads. The Germans were careful where possible not to antagonize the local people unnecessarily; collaborators were appointed to key positions in Holland and Denmark, Pétain advocated a policy of submission, and in Norway Vidkun Quisling became Prime Minister, thereafter lending his name to all those willing to work alongside the occupying forces.

Nazi policies varied from country to country; in Poland, for instance, where there was a longstanding tradition of anti-semitism, the deportation of two million Jews aroused little public reaction from the rest of the population. On the other hand, in countries such as France and Holland the Germans' Jewish policies were applied rather more discreetly. But always there was the same playing up of national and religious differences. In Belgium the Flemings were set against the Walloons; the Czechs versus the Slovaks; the Bulgarians were forcibly settled in Thrace and encouraged to live off the local Greek population; and in Yugoslavia the Serbs, Croats and Slovenes were encouraged to pay off old, bitter scores against each other. Thus the puppet dictator the Germans installed in Croatia, a Dr Pavelic, ordered the massacre of all Serbs, whether they be men, women or children. Over half a million people perished.[1]

The German policy of reprisals also hampered the growth of resistance in the early years. The death of a single German in Yugoslavia meant the massacre of a hundred Slavs, or in Poland of a thousand Poles. The occupying regime possessed a monopoly of weapons and ammunition, and it was difficult for resisters to obtain comparably effective equipment. Even when a few supplies were parachuted in, often the Germans' sophisticated detection devices enabled them to intercept such drops. The natural focus for any resistance had also been obliterated, as almost the first acts of the new authorities were to outlaw trade unions, strikes and political parties, and many newspapers and universities were also shut down. The churches' attitudes towards fascism, and particularly the treatment of Jews, remained ambiguous and inconsistent – especially those of the Roman Catholic hierarchy – although numerous individual priests and members of the clergy lost their lives aiding the resistance.

Finally, a further factor hampering the development of the anti-fascist struggle was the existence of the Nazi – Soviet Pact, in consequence of which communist parties everywhere denounced the war as 'imperialist', standing on the sidelines and keeping their hands clean. However, it is dangerous to make too many generalizations. Thousands of rank-and-file Communist Party members disregarded the official 'line' and organized some of the first acts of resistance. In France, for instance, they planned the strike of 100,000 miners between May and June of 1941 and also the mass strikes of February 1941 in Amsterdam against the treatment of deported Jews.

The Nazi 'new order' decreed that the resources and wealth of the occupied countries were to be used for the greater glory of the Third Reich, and therefore industries were expropriated, property looted, and food, minerals and other resources transferred to Germany. A typical case was that of Holland where, by the end of 1941, one-third of Dutch industry worked directly for the Nazis and half of the country's fruit and vegetables was exported to Germany. Another example comes from Greece, where the loss of the requisitioned wheat resulted in the gradual starvation of many Greeks. The consequences, graphically described by the Ankara correspondent of the *New York Times* in February 1942, demonstrated just what the 'new order' meant:

An average of 500 residents of Athens and the Piraeus are dying daily; the principal streets of the Greek capital are littered with dead and dying; the crowds of beggars are growing in numbers daily; virtually all children are developing the wasted, bent rickety legs and swollen bellies of incipient starvation.[2]

Throughout Europe it was a similar story, and the shortage of food was compounded by cholera and typhoid epidemics.

The slow but steady growth of resistance movements quickened as the implications of German occupation made themselves clearer, but geographical factors also played an important part. In Yugoslavia the Partisans under Tito were soon in action from 1940, sheltering in that region's abundant mountains and woods. In Poland the harshness of the Nazi regime rapidly prompted an underground movement which by the end of 1940 had organized its own law courts and universities, hiding in the forests and marshes when the Gestapo tried to locate them. In Norway too the long coastline enabled groups of people to come and go relatively safely, and the Greek terrain assisted the indigenous guerilla movement which harassed the enemy, striking at vital communication points such as railway bridges. All over Europe civilians initiated their own particular forms of resistance. Industry was sabotaged, a permanent 'go slow' introduced, trains derailed, underground newspapers were read and handed on – in France alone there were 70 such papers in existence by 1943 with a circulation of nearly one-and-a-half million per month – and national days celebrated in a manner which left little doubt about the peoples' assessment of military occupation.[3]

The German reaction was always vicious. In Paris by mid-1942 an average of 45 people were being executed each day, and often eyes were gouged out and legs and arms snapped before the shootings took place; at Uzice in Yugoslavia Panzer tanks ran over the wounded Partisans (as members of the resistance were known) in the fields; and at Lidice in Czechoslovakia the entire village was razed to the ground and every adult massacred as a reprisal for the assassination of the German commander Heydrich in May 1942. But overshadowing all these atrocities was the 'final solution' – the slaughtering of six million Jews and other 'undesirables' including gypsies, homosexuals, 'coloured' people and political dissidents.

But despite these terrible actions the resistance movements gained in strength and the biggest impetus came when the Germans launched 'Operation Barbarossa' in June 1941, the attack on the Soviet Union which Hitler in his book *Mein Kampf* had pledged to execute.

Although Stalin had received repeated warnings of an imminent

German attack, by the summer of 1941 he was desperately hoping to avert a war until the next year, thereby gaining a few more precious months in which to modernize and expand the Red army. Many of the problems of the Soviet forces, revealed in the winter war against Finland when they lost 1,600 tanks and over 800 aircraft, were the direct responsibility of Stalin himself. The wholesale purges of the late 1930s had not spared the army. Three out of 5 marshals, 11 deputy commissars of defence, 13 out of 15 army commanders, every one of the military district commanders active in May 1937, and in all some 35,000 officers were executed, imprisoned or dismissed, leaving the armed forces desperately short of experienced leaders. Furthermore most commanders were still in the process of discarding their preoccupation with the cavalry tactics of the Russian Civil War for the modern emphasis on armoured offensives. Together with this the Red army was deficient in radio equipment, and a mechanized corps had only been introduced in July 1940. Stalin was afraid of provoking the Germans in any way, and he had stuck by the provisions of the Nazi–Soviet Pact which had included supplying the German regime with raw materials and food. Throughout 1941 he rejected deployments of Soviet troops that could possibly be construed as provocative; which meant that on the night of 21 June 1941, the Red army was disorganized and out of position.

On 22 June 1941 the Germans launched their offensive with 3,400,000 men, a force spearheaded by Panzer tank divisions and motor corps and supported by contingents of troops from Rumania, Hungary, Slovakia, Finland, Italy and Spain. The Soviet defence was caught completely off-guard; much of the air force was destroyed on its airfields, and by the end of the first day some German divisions had advanced up to 60 miles.

Not surprisingly several Soviet commanders panicked and for a few days Stalin himself appeared numbed and incapable of taking control. But then, on 3 July, he broadcast an appeal to the Soviet nation, calling on them to display sacrifice and heroism in fighting this 'great patriotic war' for the defence of their homeland. He also enunciated the 'scorched earth' tactics which were later to prove so crucial in denying resources and equipment to the invaders:

In case of a forced retreat...all rolling stock must be
evacuated, the enemy must not be left a single engine, a
single railway car, a single pound of grain or gallon of
fuel. The collective farmers must drive all their cattle and
turn over their grain to the safe keeping of the authorities
for transportation to the rear. All valuable property, including metals, grain and fuel, that cannot be withdrawn,
must be destroyed without fail.[4]

The tragedy of this self-destruction lay in the fact that it entailed
the deliberate obliteration of those economic gains which the Soviet
Union had so painfully achieved in the 1930s.

It was here, on the Eastern Front, that the fate of the Second
World War was decided. The Red army always faced the great
bulk of the German forces — most of the time four-fifths of their
men and never less than three-quarters. For example, within 50
days of the start of 'Barbarossa' the Germans had lost nearly
400,000 men; between September 1939 and May 1941, during
the entire Polish, Norwegian, French, North African and Balkan
campaigns, they lost but half that number. The Russians too sustained devastating losses — at Kiev they suffered 600,000 casualties
and at the Battle of Smolensk over 300,000 of their troops were
taken prisoner. By the end of July the Red army's 29 armoured
divisions had been reduced to just nine in number. Their problems
were exacerbated by the need to evacuate vital industrial plant further
eastwards in order for it not to fall into enemy hands. In an operation of remarkable efficiency over 1,500 industrial concerns, including 1,360 major armaments factories, were transferred between July and November 1941.

The German forces continued their march onward, but the
Soviet command had now been reorganized under Marshal Zhukov
and the Red army halted the German advance towards Moscow
by September 1941. Although Kiev, Odessa and Kharkov had fallen
and large parts of the Ukraine, the Crimea and the Donbas were
in enemy hands, fierce Russian resistance and German troop ex-
haustion were slowing down their rate of progress. The snow and
the mud rendered many roads impassable and retreating Soviet
troops always destroyed the railways, forcing the Germans to construct

makeshift lines of communication. And then there was the bitter cold, as Guderian explicitly recalled in his memoirs:

> There is nothing more dramatic in military history than the stunning cold on the German army. The men had great-coats and jackboots. The only additional clothing they had received consisted of a scarf and a pair of gloves. In the line, weapons were unserviceable and the tank motors had to be warmed up for 12 hours before the machines could get going. One hideous detail is that many men, while satisfying the call of nature, died when their anuses froze.

The German offensive on Moscow was beaten back between October 1941 and January 1942, but Leningrad remained under siege, a disastrous Soviet offensive at Kharkov had cost well over 300,000 men and now Stalingrad in the south was threatened. Zhukov again took control, and by November 1942 the German forces under Paulus were encircled. Over 200,000 of their troops had perished before Paulus surrendered in January 1943, enabling the Red army to capture another 90,000 prisoners, a figure that included 24 generals and 2,500 other officers. Stalingrad was the turning-point of the war, a crushing defeat which destroyed the myth of Third Reich invincibility. As Liddell Hart has written: 'Morally even more than materially, the disaster of that army at Stalingrad had an effect from which the German army never recovered.'[5] There was still a long way to go, millions more deaths and atrocities yet to be perpetrated, but German strength was now clearly on the ebb.

Throughout the rest of Europe the struggle on the Eastern Front brought further hope to the anti-fascist struggle. The upsurge of admiration for the Soviet Union helped to prevent the numerous ideas floated throughout the war for the Allied to implement a 'separate peace' in the West and then unleash their forces too on the Bolshevik regime, from ever getting off the ground. One early example of such a plan was the mission of Rudolph Hess to Britain in June 1941, which proved to be entirely abortive because public opinion was overwhelmingly behind the fight against Hitler and the Nazis.

A further reason for the upsurge in Soviet popularity was that the enormous Soviet losses contrasted with British and American reluctance to open a 'Second Front' in the West against Germany. In addition, communists everywhere now played a prominent part in the underground. All over Europe the Resistance movement was expanding in size and influence, as three cases demonstrate: France, Yugoslavia and Greece.

In France the situation was at first confused by the existence of Pétain's Vichy regime, but in November 1942 the Germans decided to occupy the whole country. The French Resistance was divided between those who fought from outside the country — such as de Gaulle's 'Free French' in London from 1941 — and those active within the country itself. In May 1943 these latter groups merged to form the National Council of Resistance. The Council was growing rapidly in power and actually found itself helped by German policies. In 1943 the conscription of labour and deportations to Germany were stepped up, and many of those directed to go fled to join the underground.

By September 1943 the Resistance was strong enough to have liberated Corsica, but always such successes went hand in hand with disasters. At Vercors a premature rising led to a pitched battle with the Germans — something that the practitioners of guerilla war with their tactics of short, sharp and furtive assaults always tried to avoid — and 700 members of the Resistance were killed. Reprisals continued: 700 people were massacred at Oradour-sur-Plane in June 1944, nearly half of whom were children.

It is difficult to estimate just how many participated in the French Resistance, especially as the degree of activity varied from hiding a downed RAF pilot to derailing a troop train. There were perhaps 100,000 maquis by 1944 and some 30,000 in Brittany alone, and their operations continually harried and weakened the Germans. Between January and March 1943, for instance, the underground claimed 150 derailings, 180 locomotives carrying material and troops destroyed, and 800 members of the Wehrmacht killed or wounded.[6]

The Resistance movement in Yugolavia was split between the Cetniks and the Partisans. The former were led by Mihailovic and the latter by Tito, a fiercely determined communist who had worked

in Moscow in the 1930s, survived the purges and was now drawing upon the guerilla tradition which the peoples of Yugoslavia
had for centuries practised against invaders. Mihailovic, however,
soon stopped fighting the Germans, preferring to bide his time
and wait to deal with the communists at the end of the war, and
thus it was the Partisans who bore the main brunt of the struggle.
Tito insisted on complete racial equality within the movement — an
especially progressive order at a time when the fascists had set
Croats, Serbs and Slavs at each other's throats — and the disciplined
Partisans never requisitioned food or supplies from the peasants
but always paid for them. By the beginning of 1944 the Partisans
numbered 250,000 — a quarter of whom were women — and they
were tying down 15 German divisions which Hitler would have
preferred on the Eastern Front. The Germans made repeated efforts
to encircle and destroy the Partisans but their skilful use of the
terrain, its woods, mountains and few roads, combined with the
overwhelming support of the population who often took appalling risks in helping them, enabled Tito and his forces to remain
at large.[7]

In Greece there were also two partisan movements: ELAS,
which was a broadly-based body that by 1944 had 30,000 guerillas,
and EDES, led by Zervas, a quarter of ELAS's size and, like the
Cetniks, not averse to deals and truces with the occupying
authorities. EAM, on the other hand, the political body which had
set up ELAS in September 1941, was firmly rooted in popular support and claimed a membership of more than two million. It
organized a number of civilian strikes and demonstrations against
the quisling Tsolakoglou regime. ELAS continually harassed the
Germans; the Gorgopotamos bridge on the Athens — Salonica
railway, a route on which Rommel depended for his supplies, was
blown up in November 1942; in the summer of 1943 the Asopos
bridge in central Greece was also destroyed, as were further bridges
on the Athens — Salonica line and an important tunnel in
Thessaly.[8]

Elsewhere, as you would expect, the extent and nature of
resistance varied but was never less than important. The flat terrain
hampered the development of an underground in Holland and
Belgium so they concentrated on intelligence gathering; in Norway

the Milorg numbered over 30,000 by mid-1944 and fully extended 17 German divisions; Hoxha led a sizeable Resistance movement in mountainous Albania that tied down 20 German divisions;
the Italian Partisans numbered over 150,000, and by the spring
of 1944 the Polish Resistance could call upon 400,000 people.
But perhaps the most successful of all the partisan organizations
were those active behind enemy lines inside the Soviet Union,
especially in the forests and swamps of Belorussia and the nor-
thern Ukraine. By mid-1942 the Soviet Partisans were putting 200
trains out of action a month, and their activities were co-ordinated
by a central staff in Moscow which set up training schools and
supplied equipment.

An important point to stress about all the resistance movements
is their indigenous and native character, the genuine response of
ordinary men and women to the consequences of fascist occupation. They grew spontaneously and at first in a disorganized fashion,
relying almost entirely on their own wit and ingenuity. Both the
Soviet Union and Britain were in the early years fighting for their
own survival and therefore had few supplies to spare. The British
did establish a Special Operations Executive (SOE) responsible for
sabotage in enemy-occupied territory, and the work of some of
these men and women sent in to join and advise the resistance
groups was invaluable. But not all of this assistance was entirely
disinterested. In fact the most significant contributions of the two
major European powers lay in the work of the BBC Foreign Service and of Radio Moscow—stations broadcasting throughout
Europe and nurturing what has been termed 'the renaissance of
hope' exemplified by the Resistance.

The driving force behind the resistance movements was the
surge of nationalism directed against the occupying powers, but
intermingled with this mood was the widespread desire for
economic and social change. Should people be prepared to risk
their lives for a return of the injustices of the interwar years, for
a return to the old order of poverty, unemployment and the brutal
regimes led by such as Horthy and Metaxas, Kings Boris and Carol?
No, of course not, and the anti-fascist struggle inexorably shifted
the political spectrum leftwards as the Resistance initiated new
and more radical forms of organization. In Greece, for instance,

People's Committees were elected in areas liberated by ELAS, a procedure paralleled by that in Yugoslavia. In Italy Committees of National Liberation created in the major cities encouraged the development of workers' councils and agricultural co-operatives, and in Poland the underground constituted what was in effect a state within a state. Everywhere the Resistance was distinguished by its democratic character, with men and women participating on an equal basis and discussing fully decisions and tasks to be undertaken. The writer and member of the Resistance Jean-Paul Sartre best described this sense of community in an article about the underground written just after the Liberation of Paris:

> There is no army in the world where one can find such equality of risk for the soldier and the general. And this is why the Resistance was a true democracy; for the soldier as for his chief, the same danger, the same relaxation, the same total responsibility, the same absolute liberty in discipline. Thus, in the shadow and in the blood, a republic has been constituted, the strongest of all republics.[9]

By the winter of 1943−4 it became increasingly evident that the fight would be won, and the Resistance began to issue programmes concerning postwar problems and reconstruction. At Jajce, Yugoslavia in November 1943 the Partisans set up a parliament, issuing a manifesto which promised self-government for the provinces, national self-determination and economic and social reforms. In France the Committee of National Resistance produced a set of demands in March 1944 that included the establishment of the freedom of the press, equal rights, the nationalization of monopolies, the right to work and an extensive social security system as postwar priorities. EAM-ELAS insisted that there could be no return to the conditions of the Metaxas dictatorship and a plebiscite should be held regarding the future role of King George; and in Poland the Committee of National Liberation demanded wholesale land reform−in 1944 six million hectares were redistributed, with a similar process occurring in Rumania.

The Resistance movements were part of a Europe-wide struggle. They were fighting a common enemy, and in 1944 the leaders of seven Resistance organizations met at Geneva to discuss forthcoming events. A blow against the Germans in Greece or Albania helped to take some of the pressure off, say, Britain or the Soviet Union, and this prevalent internationalism was widely shared. One incident sums this up: many of the bombs dropped by the Luftwaffe in the autumn of 1940−1 on Britain were made in Czech factories but did not explode−inside the bombs were found messages from Czech workers explaining that the sabotage was their contribution to the Allied cause.[10] The Resistance was a revival of hope and dignity, of a belief and confidence in the ability of men and women to create a better world−a genuinely European experience, not so much in itself the expression of a fully politicized and socialist continent but rather the vital platform from which gains could be secured. Of course the strength of these radical moods varied from country to country but they were powerful everywhere and in some countries, such as Bulgaria, Czechoslovakia, Greece and Yugoslavia, they were tantamount to a revolutionary situation.

The Red army continued its westward march as the haemorrhaging of German strength accelerated apace. At Kursk from July to August 1943−the greatest armoured engagement in world history−the Germans lost half a million men and 2,000 tanks. There was no way they could recover from such losses. In the Pacific war, although the Japanese had completely surprised the US Navy at Pearl Harbor in December 1941, American economic and military superiority was beginning to tell.

In Europe the Americans were continuing to discuss the opening of a Second Front with Britain−and D-Day did not finally take place until June 1944−but they were fighting their way up Italy following the seizure of Sicily by the Allies in August 1943, immeasurably aided by the Partisans, who prevented the retreating Germans from also implementing a 'scorched earth' policy.

The final German threat came with the Ardennes offensive of late 1944 (known as the Battle of the Bulge), a last desperate gamble which caught the British and American forces off-guard. It ended when Stalin, responding to Churchill's frantic pleas, ordered the Red army to quicken its advance and by doing so split the German defences.

The ebb of German strength heightened the importance of the high-level conferences held between Roosevelt, Churchill and Stalin, ostensibly to discuss the shape of the postwar world. All three men possessed enormous power over the lives and futures of millions, and their wheeling and dealing provides a vivid contrast with the popular grassroots initiatives elsewhere in Europe. Roosevelt had always distrusted what he regarded as the imperial pretensions of Churchill, and joint statements such as the Atlantic Charter of August 1941 expressed American beliefs in national self-determination. Churchill however made it clear in the House of Commons that such sentiments did not apply to India. Stalin likewise never forgot Churchill's role in the Russian Civil War. His suspicions that the delay in establishing a Second Front lay in the wish to see Germany and the Soviet Union batter themselves defenceless first were fuelled by the numerous and quite open Nazi plans circulating urging a separate peace in the West (this was the objective behind von Stauffenburg's plot to assassinate Hitler in 1944).

Stalin's cynicism in dealing with the fate of millions of people was matched only by that of Churchill when, at their momentous meeting in Moscow during October 1944, they discussed their respective 'spheres of influences' after the war. Churchill supplies a graphic account in his own *History of the Second World War*. He scribbled on a piece of paper his suggestions that the Russians should have 90 per cent influence in Rumania, 10 per cent in Greece, 75 per cent in Bulgaria, and 50 per cent in Yugoslavia and Hungary, the remaining percentages to be controlled by Britain:

> I pushed this across to Stalin...Then he took his blue pencil and made a large tick upon it, and passed it back to us...At length I said: 'Might it not be thought rather cynical if it seemed we had disposed of these issues...in such an offhand manner? Let us burn the paper.' 'No, you keep it,' said Stalin.[11]

These were the 'spheres of influence' which, with the agreement of President Roosevelt and the Americans, were confirmed at the

Yalta Conference in February 1945.

' As the Red army hurtled forward, so Stalin's hand was strengthened as he established governments in liberated territories sympathetic to the Soviet Union. This was hardly surprising, nor was he alone in this. The American administration in Italy disarmed the Resistance, appointed their own nominees to office and stipulated that there should be no 'political activity' until the end of the war. The man appointed to implement this policy, Lord Rennell, typified that British establishment of the 1930s which had so mishandled Hitler.

But really what was coming to the fore, now that the unanimity imposed by a common enemy was breaking up, was a demonstration of the basic division between those who wished to minimize the radical political and social change engendered by the war, and those desirous of utilizing it in the construction of a fairer postwar world. Such tensions, though masked, had been apparent from early on. It was the split between de Gaulle's Free French and the Committee of National Resistance; between Mihailovic's Cetniks and Tito's Partisans; EAM-ELAS and EDES in Greece; and in Poland between Bor-Komorowski's 'Secret Army' and the 'People's Guard'. It was in Greece that the frictions first erupted in violence, where the collision between popular aspiration and diplomatic 'realpolitik' was most sharp.

By the end of 1944 EAM-ELAS controlled the greater part of Greece. Churchill, who in particular advocated the re-establishment of the traditional regime of king and 'law and order', watched the activities of the Partisans in horror. The British Mission to ELAS had attempted to minimize their power and, in the words of its leader Brigadier Myers, prevented ELAS's total victory. Churchill telegraphed to Ambassador Leeper and General Scobie, the commander of the British troops, that they should not be afraid to use force if necessary to put down any real or perceived 'unrest'. On 3 December 1944 a peaceful protest march was held in Athens. The police opened fire, killing 28 people and seriously wounding another 150. Demonstrations against 'bloody Sunday' gave the authorities further excuses for moving against ELAS; Churchill admitted in the House of Commons that he directed General Scobie 'to use whatever force might be necessary to drive out and extirpate the ELAS bands by which the capital has become infested.'[12] Remember that this is Churchill talking about the Partisans who for nearly five years had fought tirelessly and heroically against the Germans whilst King George, the man who condoned the Metaxas dictatorship, and his supporters, remained safely in exile. The *Times* correspondent on the spot expressed his views in unequivocal terms: 'The presence of our troops served only to associate Britain with what is everywhere condemned as "fascist" action.'

The events of December 1944 in Athens heralded the advent of the Greek Civil War, in effect an attempt by the British to beat back the phoenix rising out of the ashes of occupation. Ernest Bevin, a member of the coalition government and a future foreign secretary, defended the Churchill government's conduct at the Labour Party Conference by asserting that 'the British Empire cannot abandon its position in the Mediterranean'. The civil war totally rent the country, setting Greek against Greek and destroying the popular anti-fascist consensus so painfully constructed during the war. 'Partisan' became a dirty word, labour unions were destroyed and thousands of political prisoners incarcerated on distant islands. Stalin, true to the Moscow agreement, left them to their fate. The events in Greece were also a portent of things to come.

In April 1945 American and Soviet troops met on the Elbe, and their hearty welcome of each other somehow symbolized the spirit and aspirations of wartime internationalism, however tarnished by civil war in Greece. The Germans surrendered on 7 May, Hitler having committed suicide a few days before. In the Far East the Americans dropped two atom bombs at Hiroshima and Nagasaki with devastating effect, and Japan capitulated on 2 September 1945.

There are two major themes running through this chapter: the significance of the Resistance, and the contribution of the Soviet Union to the victory over the Germans. With the onset of the Cold War in the late 1940s, both of these facts have invariably been minimized or downgraded in Western Europe for political reasons. It is worth quoting the remarks of two people, both generals and conservatives, made actually at the time.

First of all General Eisenhower, the leader of the Allied forces, had this to say about the Resistance in May 1945:

I consider that the disruption of enemy rail communications, the harassing of German road moves and the continual and increasing strain placed upon the German war economy and internal security services throughout occupied Europe by the organized forces of Resistance, played a very considerable part in our complete and final victory.[13]

The other testimony comes from Field Marshall Montgomery in a speech he delivered in Moscow in January 1947, a time when the wartime alliances had virtually disintegrated:

In my speech I referred to the great war effort of Russia. Britain had gone through some bad times in 1940, 1941 and 1942, and for a long time we fought alone against the combined might of Germany and Italy. But we were lucky in that the German armies failed to carry the land war into England, and we were saved from having our homeland destroyed by the fascist hordes. Not so with Russia. While Britain and America were gathering their strength, the German armies overran and ravished the homelands of Russia, causing terrific destruction and great loss of life. Britain and America in those early days could do little to help, except to supply equipment by sea; Russia had to bear, almost unaided, the full onslaught of Germany on land. We British would never forget what Russia went through; she had suffered more severely than any other nation.[14]

For five years Europe and the rest of the world had suffered all the ravages of the most destructive and murderous war in human history. In what sort of condition was Europe by 1945?

5. The aftermath

An inventory of Europe in the summer of 1945 would have shown a shattered and mutilated continent. In all some 55 million people had died, one half of whom were civilians. At one end of the scale the Soviet Union had lost 20 million dead and Poland 8 million, with Britain towards the other end numbering 325,000 dead. The fact that it was a world war and not just confined to Europe is seen by the 12 million dead in China and three million in Japan — the United States saw 250,000 of its people killed.

A further eight million refugees or 'displaced persons' were all over the roads of Europe, and cities such as Warsaw, Dresden and Leningrad had been virtually razed to the ground. With transport, schools and hospitals destroyed, Europe had been thrown back decades. Both wheat and industrial output in 1945 were less than one-third of 1939 levels. In Holland, for example, thousands of acres of fertile soil had been flooded with salt water as the retreating Germans dynamited the sea walls. Even Britain, which had fortunately been spared the horrors of occupation, found that one-quarter of the national wealth and two-thirds of its export trade had been wiped out.

As the Allies made their way deep into Germany, they came across further evidence of the degradation and inhuman depths to which fascism could reduce people. The Red army had reached the concentration camp of Maidanek in the summer of 1944, and with them was the *Sunday Times* correspondent Alexander Werth. The following describes just part of what he stumbled across at the crematorium:

The place stank, not violently, but it stank of decomposition.

I looked down. My shoes were white with human dust, and the concrete floor around the ovens was strewn with parts of charred human skeletons. Here was a whole chest with its ribs, here a piece of skull, here a lower jaw with a molar on either side, nothing but sockets in between.[1]

At first the BBC and several newspapers refused Werth's articles, unable to believe that such atrocities could have taken place.

Later on, as camps like Auschwitz, Dachau and Belsen were evacuated, such accounts and findings became the norm. An all-party group of British MPs visited Buchenwald and their report, written by Tom Driberg, was published as a government white paper. One paragraph is about the dysentry hut:

This hut was about 8 feet long by 24 feet wide, estimates of its normal sick population varied from 700 to 1,300. Four, 5 or 6 men including those who had undergone operations (performed without anaesthetics by prison doctors on a crude operating table at one end of the hut, in full view of the other patients), had regularly to lie in each of the small shelf cubicles. Here, too, there were no mattresses. The excreta of the dysentry patients dripped down from tier to tier. If the living were strong enough, they pushed the dead out into the gangway. Each night the dead were thrown into a small annexe at one end of the hut, and each morning collected and taken in carts to the crematorium, or, if required as specimens, to the pathological laboratory of the Nazi doctors.[2]

But although such atrocities can never — and should never — be forgotten, it is important to remember that fascism was defeated, that there was a 'liberation' in every sense of the word. And reading through diaries, letters, newpapers and books of the time, again and again one is struck by the feeling of opportunity, the sense of a continent waking from a protracted nightmare. A number of examples will bring home this point, and the three people concerned came from very different backgrounds: a British officer, a German housewife and a French writer.

First of all, Major Frank Thompson, writing home from the Middle East in 1944:

> There is a spirit abroad in Europe which is freer and braver than anything that tired continent has known for centuries, and which cannot be withstood. You can, if you like, think of it in terms of politics, but it is broader and more generous than any dogma. It is the confident will of whole peoples, who have known the utmost humiliation and suffering and have triumphed over it, to build their own lives once and for all.[3]

Second, Tilli Wolff-Monckeberg, a woman opposed from the beginning to Hitler's regime, who wrote in her diary for 2 October 1945: 'slowly, very slowly, tiny, hardly visible, new seeds of hope appear in our poor destroyed Germany, how from the barren ruins signs of indomitable fresh life are peeping through.'[4] And finally Albert Camus, a member of the Resistance: 'During all the time when we were obstinately and silently serving our country, we never lost sight of an idea and a hope, forever present in us — the idea and hope of Europe.'[5]

The war — the anti-fascist war — had brought in its wake seismic changes. Economically, there had been the militarization of industry, 'total war', bombing, war damage and the much greater role played by governments. Socially, the commmon struggle — despite many divisions and disagreements — had engendered collective responses on egalitarian lines, and these impulses lived on in the hopes of a fair system of postwar reconstruction. Politically, many of the traditional institutions of authority — landowner, industrialist and church — were heavily weakened by their somewhat accommodating attitude towards fascism. Together, this meant that old, familiar landmarks had been obliterated and, as one observer wrote at the time, 'We are like men exploring the earth after a cataclysm, but with the old maps.'[6]

In many ways the ferment of Europe reflected the human dignity and self-respect with which the Resistance had countered fascism, and no one wished to return to the 1930s. De Gaulle wrote succintly of the evident changes when he returned to France in 1944:

'Their [the people's] aversion for the structure of the past was exacerbated by poverty, concentrated by the Resistance and exalted by the Liberation.'[7]

Only rarely does such a mood arise, as Neal Ascherson has written in his book on Poland:

> In this association of liberation with revolution, of resistance with social equality, the Poles were not of course alone but part of the huge revival of political energy that was experienced by almost every nation in Europe. We have no name for this episode of history. It lasted roughly from 1943 to 1948. In its power and universality, it was almost a repetition of the continental wave of revolutions in 1848, just a century before, and, like that 'Springtime of Nations', its power derived from the confluence of armed struggle for national independence with ideologies of social and economic change.[8]

Britain at this time provides a good illustration of the radical transformation of attitudes and opinions since the 1930s. On the one hand it differed from the rest of Europe in that it had not been occupied, and thus many of its traditional institutions remained virtually intact. On the other, it too had felt, as we saw in chapter 3, the consequences of the 'people's war'.

The electoral truce during the war years helped to mask many of the changes then taking place, although polls in the *News Chronicle* and Mass-Observation surveys indicated which way the wind was blowing. The Labour Party leaders themselves, their prestige enchanced by their role in the coalition government, remained insulated from rank-and-file pressure and their future plans betrayed an incongruous sense of timidity. The 1944 conference witnessed an eruption of discontent at the caution of the party's programme, with delegates passing a resolution against the express wishes of the National Executive Committee which called for 'the transfer to public ownership of the land, large-scale building, heavy industry and all forms of banking, transport and fuel and power', together with the directive that these should be 'democratically controlled'.

The Conservative Party entered the election campaign of 1945 in a parlous state. The party organization had disintegrated, Churchill's distaste for domestic isssues had inhibited policy-making, and the electorate firmly identified the Conservatives with the appeasement and mass unemployment of the 1930s. Books such as Simon Haxey's *Tory MP* and Tom Wintringham's *Your MP* published the many incriminating statements by Conservative MPs in the past on such questions as Hitler, Mussolini and the means test. The Party's strategy for the election relied heavily on the prestige and popularity of Churchill himself—their manifesto was entitled *Mr Churchill's Declaration of Policy to the Electors*, overlooking the fact that this was solely rooted in his actions as a war leader.

Both Conservative and Labour manifestos—the latter was called *Let Us Face the Future*—showed many overlaps, especially concerning the need for a massive housing programme, the introduction of a health service and a national insurance scheme; but as the election campaign got under way tempers quickened. Everywhere huge public meetings were held, speakers closely examined and political literature devoured by the crowds. One observer, Harold Nicolson, estimated that 'class feeling and class resentment are very strong', not surprisingly perhaps when Churchill suggested that no socialist system could be established without a political police and Labour would have to resort to some form of Gestapo. The *Evening Standard* went further, printing the pictures of Labour's National Executive Committee, a thoroughly mild and inoffensive looking bunch, under the caption 'These People Want to Be Dictators. Study their Faces'![9]

The election results were announced on 26 and 27 July 1945, and the news that the Labour Party had won 393 seats compared with the Conservative total of 213 was greeted with jubilation: bonfires were lit and people danced in the streets with joy. Two groups in particular had voted by a sizeable majority for Labour, the young and those in the forces.

Overall the mood was summed up by the new Chancellor of the Exchequer, Hugh Dalton, who noted in his diary—expressing what much of Europe felt—'That first sensation, tingling and triumphant, was of a new society to be built, and we had the power to build it. There was exhilaration among us, joy and hope, determination and confidence. We felt exalted, dedicated, walking on air, walking with destiny.'[10]

Elsewhere in Europe the results of elections further reflected the vast social and political changes which had swept through the continent. The beneficiaries of this were the various socialist parties but more particularly the communists, who were seen as having played the major part in the Resistance movement and also benefited from their association with the much-vaunted Soviet Union.

In France, the Communist Party numbered more than 900,000 members by June 1945, and their strength was indicated in the general election when they amassed over five million votes or 25 per cent of the electorate; the Socialists gained four-and-a-half million or 23 per cent, as did the Christian Democrats. Although de Gaulle was the Prime Minister and averse to radical changes, he had no option but largely to acquiesce. Gas, coal, insurance, electricity, Renault, the Bank of France and most important private banks — all these concerns were taken into public ownership. Social insurance laws were passed in April 1946 and pensions greatly increased.

In Italy the strength of the Resistance enabled them to liberate well over 100 towns without Allied support, and a correspondingly powerful anti-fascist coalition was formed under Bonomi late in 1944 with four communists as members. By December 1945 the Communist Party had 1.7 million members, and in the elections of 1946 — the first free elections since 1922 — they won 104 seats, the Socialists 115 and the Christain Democrats 207. In June 1946 a referendum determined that the monarchy should be abolished and a republic introduced.

In smaller countries too a similar process was under way. Austria, for example, saw the People's Party secure a majority at the election and nationalize many industrial enterprises. In Norway the Labour Party formed the new government. On the other side of the continent comparable changes were taking place as coalition governments in Yugoslavia, Bulgaria, Rumania, Hungary and Poland began their efforts to sweep away some of the debris accumulated in the interwar years. In fact, as Alfred Grosser has commented:

The surprise at the victory of the Labour Party in the July 1945 British elections can be ascribed to the failure to recognize a profound transnational movement. Everywhere, in France, Denmark, Italy, Germany and Belgium, a push towards the left was taking place...To the extent socialism can be defined, the Europe of 1945/46 was certainly right to call itself socialist.[11]

Although this period was the high-water mark of European radicalism, of popular idealism and enthusiasm, it would be foolish to exaggerate this mood. Traditional ideas and institutions had been badly shaken but not totally obliterated, and they still retained a residual loyalty. In Italy in 1946, for instance, over 10 million people had voted for the retention of the monarchy despite its intimate links with Mussolini's regime.

Similarly the legacy of the war was not by any means entirely beneficial. The economic disruption posed severe constraints and the bitter anti-semitism stirred up by the Germans was not likely just to vanish into thin air. But above all this, the consensus imposed on the Allies by the common war against fascism was beginning to splinter and break up — and the consequences of this were deeply important and of permanent significance.

6. Britain in the late Forties

The Labour Party had experienced a heady triumph in the July 1945 election. MPs from the younger generation were returned for the first time and at the beginning of the first session they celebrated by singing the Red Flag. Conservative MPs were outraged but also worried by the self-confidence of this demonstration; one of them, Oliver Lyttelton, wrote in his memoirs: 'My complacency melted in a minute. I began to fear for my country.' The Labour government's leaders, however, were rather more realistic, as Herbert Morrison noted that 'although mildly disturbed... these youngsters still had to absorb the atmosphere of the House. But I recognized that it was largely first-day high spirits.'[1]

There was little doubt that the country at large was in the mood for, and expected, a far-reaching series of reforms. A Gallup Poll after the election found that 56 per cent reckoned the electorate had voted for sweeping changes. The war had both revealed the weaknesses of private enterprise – particularly its concern with profit before social needs – and the valuable tasks that government intervention could fulfil, and the Labour administration began work with great energy. In 1946 alone eight major pieces of legislation were placed on the statute book.

The government's economic policy, as elsewhere in Europe, focused on the extension of public ownership. The mines and railways were two basic utilities that by 1945 were thoroughly dilapidated, and not just as as result of the war. Britain's mines had operated at a loss for years, run by many different companies with low wages and an horrific accident record. By the end of the war even the coal-owners recognized the need for some form of centralized body: the *Economist* commented soon after the government came to power: 'Support for the principle of public ownership of the mines is now very wide, extending probably to two-and-a-half of the three parties.'

As for the railways, although the numerous companies had been slimmed down to the 'big four' in 1921, this led to little modernization—for instance, the use of diesel engines was virtually unknown before the war. During the war itself the four independent companies had proved unable to cope with the increased flow of freight and a system of centralization was initiated from 1941. Here too the fact of public ownership had virtually been settled already and there was little opposition to the idea. In fact, as Attlee recalled in his memoirs: 'Of all our nationalization proposals, only Iron and Steel aroused much feeling, perhaps because hopes of profit were greater here than elsewhere.'[2]

But the question still to be faced centred on how nationalization was to be carried out. The famous Clause 4, an integral part of Labour's 1918 constitution and still printed today on each party member's card, calls for the 'common ownership of the means of production, distribution, and exhange, and the best obtainable system of popular administration and control of each industry or service'. However, neither of the two previous Labour governments of 1924 and 1929—31 had made significant progress towards executing this objective.

One strand that weaves its way through this topic is the debate cencerning workers' control. For instance Clement Attlee in his book *The Will and the Way to Socialism*, published in 1935, declared that 'workers' control is an essential part of the new order', but ten years on such ideas had been allowed to go by the board. In the main this was because of Herbert Morrison, the domineering figure who favoured the public corporation approach and justified nationlization on grounds of economic efficiency, not as a step towards socialism. It was Morrison who was responsible for overseeing the passage of the new government's nationalization Bills.[3]

In any case, the Labour Party was now to pay the price for its meagre policy-making of the 1930s. Manny Shinwell was the new Minister of Fuel and he has recalled how little guidance he had about public ownership of coalmining: 'I enquired whether

any documents or blueprints were available at Labour Party headquarters. None was available apart from resolutions advocating
public ownership carried at frequent conferences, and a few pamphlets... presented in general terms.'[4] Because of this, the
Labour government had little idea of the amount of compensation
which should be paid to former owners for their assets. The figures
turned out to be extremely generous: £164 million for the mines,
nearly £1,000 million for the railways, and later on £540 million
for electricity and £265 million for the gas industry. Often the
former owners were only too glad to be rid of loss-making
ventures.[5]

The Coal Industry Nationalization Act was passed in 1946,
and as well as dealing with the matter of compensation it also
established the National Coal Board (NCB). The composition of
this board reflected the dominance of the old private coal-
owners—Lord Hyndley for example, the new chairman, had
formerly been chairman of the largest private group of
collieries—and there was no provision for direct miner representation on any of the NCB committees above pit level.

The Transport Act of 1946 transferred into state ownership
the railways, canals and most long-distance road haulage, setting
up the Transport Commission. Despite the protracted attempts of
the National Union of Railwaymen to introduce some measure of
industrial democracy, relations between management and
workforce remained identical to those under private ownership.
Neither did the government obtain a unified transport policy, simply
because separate boards administered the rail and road systems
under a directive to compete against each other.

Other measures of nationalization passed by the government
were those relating to the Bank of England in 1946, electricity
in 1947 and gas in 1948. Continuity of personnel seemed to be
imperative here too. At the bank the governor, the deputy governor
and all the other leading officials were reappointed to their posts;
eight of the heads of the area gas boards had been former executives
of private gas companies.

The government's programme of nationalization suffered from
a number of common defects: all the industries taken over were
both bankrupt and backward—the unprofitable 20 per cent of British

industry. Compensation was paid on extravagant terms to companies only too glad to be rid of liabilities; and the old management structures and relationships were transferred unchanged from the private to the public sector. The editor of the *Economist*, Geoffrey Crowther, speaking to an American audience in 1949, summed up the whole experience: 'The ordinary resident in England, unless he happens to have been a shareholder in any of the expropriated companies, is unable to detect any difference whatever as a result of nationalization.'[6]

The long-term consequences of the government's methods of nationalization were just as important and loom large in the popular consciousness. Because the industries nationalized had all been on the verge of bankruptcy, a strong association was established in the public mind between socialism and bureaucratic inefficiency. It did not matter one iota that these public utilities provided a cheap infrastructure of services for the benefit of private industry. Certainly it is revealing that the Conservative Party did not commit itself at the time to any programme of denationalizing these industries.

As for the rest of the government's economic policy, at the 1945 election much had been made of the claim that the Labour Party was the natural 'planning' party in contrast to the Conservative reliance on 'market forces'. The idea of planning was in any event associated with the Soviet Union and therefore generally popular, and the war had shown the advantages of economic co-ordination. Planning was now respectable, and *Let Us Face the Future* dwelt on the prospects of a future national plan for Britain.

If this was to be executed with any degree of success then an efficient economic staff was vital. But with only 15 economists in the economic section of the cabinet and the same number of statisticians in the Central Statistical Office, government planning could be little more than a rather desperate whistling in the dark. Not surprisingly, when the government faced a convertibility crisis for the pound in 1947, Washington turned out to know rather more about what was happening than Whitehall itself. No national plan was ever produced, and when an *Economic Survey* was finally published in 1947 it revealed that planning was now seen as little more than piecemeal exhortation to private industry. Exchange controls were not introduced, so that £645 million flooded out of the country between 1947 and 1949. The advisers and consultants whom the government did appoint often came from important private firms and were thus at least implicitly hostile to Labour's approach of planning and controls — Unilever, for example, filled 90 posts in the Ministry of Food, 12 of them senior positions.[7]

By 1948 the priorities of the Attlee government had been almost reversed. It was indeed increasingly willing to intervene in one sphere, that of wages. The new Chancellor of the Exchequer, Sir Stafford Cripps, introduced a white paper in February 1948 called *Statement on Personal Incomes, Costs and Prices*. In fact the statement concentrated almost on wages, emphasizing that increases should be connected to rises in productivity. Profits and rents were scarcely mentioned — despite the fact that company profits had risen steeply since the 1930s[8] — and proposals for price controls completely absent. The statement turned out to be the prelude to a policy of wage restraint.

Cripps's budget of 1948 heralded other changes and in particular the move from direct to indirect taxation, the latter being the procedure which bears most heavily on the lower paid; it also confirmed that there was to be no widescale redistribution of wealth under this government at least. An academic economist, Dudley Seers, noted in his book *The Levelling of Incomes since 1938*, published in 1951: 'there has been no continuation after 1944 of the previous trend towards equality of distribution.'[9]

The Labour government's social reforms centred on the development of the welfare state. Although the Liberals had introduced old-age pensions in 1908 and a national health and unemployment insurance system in 1911, these constituted little more than a patchwork provision of services. During the 1920s and 1930s no administration displayed more than a passing concern in social welfare, and it was not until the consequences of 'total war' made themselves felt that basic welfare services were created; the family means test was replaced in 1941, social security benefits raised and family allowances introduced from 1945. A sequence of white papers on health, insurance and employment were published towards the end of the war, demonstrating official acceptance of the philosophy of the welfare state, and the Labour government was active in all the fields of social security, health, education, housing and jobs.

There were three major pieces of legislation on social security: the Industrial Injuries Act 1946, incorporating much of the Beveridge Report; the National Insurance Act 1946; and the National Assistance Act 1948, which established a safety-net for all those who did not fall within the scope of the 1946 acts. All three measures were a great improvement on the situation of the 1930s.

However, there were a number of flaws apparent. For instance the National Insurance Act was founded upon the contributory principle of insurance, and this meant that, unlike a non-contributory scheme which was funded out of general taxation, the labour force was already substantially paying for their benefits out of deductions from their wages. Therefore instead of those most affluent being financially responsible for social insurance — employers provided only 35 per cent, which was eligible for tax relief, and which they often passed on as price rises — a great proportion was borne by those intended to benefit from the reform. Levied at a flat rate, the contributions operated as a regressive form of taxation, nor were the benefits tied to the true cost of living.

The National Assistance Act soon found itself being increasingly used by thousands of people. The reason for this was that national insurance benefits were so meagre — reflecting a Victorian bias against anyone getting 'something' for 'nothing' — that many men and women had also to resort to means-tested national assistance. Two writers estimated later that:

the National Insurance benefits are so inadequate both in scale and scope that already by 1951 no less than two-and-a-half million people were being supported by the National Assistance Board after submitting to a means test. This is no less than one in every 20 of the population.[10]

As for the health service, there had been the same scanty provision in the 1930s as with so many other areas of welfare. Many of the books by writers like Boyd Orr, M'Gonight and Kirby, and Seebohm Rowntree's *Human Needs of Labour* demonstrated the links between poverty, infant mortality and ill-health. During the war the improvements brought about by centralization under the Emergency Medical Service had been obvious to all, and medical provision during the bombing was supplied on the simple ground of need and not that of ability to buy treatment. Building on this consensus, Aneurin Bevan pushed through the National Health Service Act in 1946, although it did not come into operation until July 1948.

Its great virtue lay in retaining the principle of medical treatment for need and not payment, although it still allowed the existence of some pay beds within the state system. Bevan found himself unable to create a full-time salaried service, and unfortunately the new health centres – which aimed to stress the values of preventive medicine within the community – were largely a victim of government cuts in the later 1940s. But these defects should not obscure the central achievements of the NHS, and the service has retained massive popular support ever since its introduction in 1948.

The Education Act of 1944 was pioneered by the Conservative MP R.A.Butler and provided the framework within which Ellen Wilkinson, the new Minister of Education, was to work. She raised the school-leaving age to 15 in 1947 but never to 16 as promised, and made no attempt to discourage private schools. Furthermore there was little support for those local education authorities not producing plans based upon a tripartite system of grammar, technical and secondary modern schools. Instead, Wilkinson and her successor George Tomlinson emphasized the virtues of the elitist grammar schools, thus ensuring that the secondary moderns would suffer from inferior resources and prestige. Although there was a sizeable increase in government expenditure on education as compared with previous administrations, the eleven-plus system meant that the supposed equality of opportunity introduced by the 1944 act came instead to reflect the existing divisions within society.[11]

Opinion polls found that the question of housing was regarded by the electorate as the most important issue of the 1945 election. Attlee immediately broke one promise by not setting up a separate Ministry of Housing, and Aneurin Bevan struggled to handle both this department and that of health. Hugh Dalton noted in his *Diaries* Bevan's supposed remark: 'I never spend more than an hour a week on housing. Housing runs itself.'[12]

The key test of the government's housing programme is the simple one of recording just how many houses were in fact built. In 1948 230,000 houses were completed as compared with the figure of 350,000 for 1938; the government was falling a long way short of its own target of 400,000 houses a year. Cuts in 1949 and 1950 further reduced the numbers, and a survey of 1951 concluded that there were 750,000 fewer houses than households—a far cry from fulfilling the election pledge about every family having a good standard of accommodation.

During the six years from 1945 in which Labour was in office a high level of employment was maintained, with the numbers of jobless restricted to about 3 per cent of the labour force, amounting in all to around 30,000 people. This was a significant improvement on the prevailing circumstances in the 1930s. However the target of full employment had become an important part of the political consensus and the Conservative Party's *Industrial Charter* of 1947 insisted they would also achieve this target if returned to office. In fact the Labour government's main grouse related to the shortage of labour available.

One problem which faced the government was that of a hostile press. Writing of these Attlee years the veteran *Sunday Times* journalist James Margach concluded: 'I have never known the press so consistently and irresponsibly political, slanted and prejudiced.'[13] Eventually the government responded by appointing a royal commission to investigate Fleet Street—which finally recommended the setting up of the Press Council—but by then the damage had been done.

In the early years the radical mood of the country seems to have remained undimmed, although some government actions were a little hard to understand. The squatters' movement in 1946 expressed a deep resentment at Labour's countenancing of untenanted luxury flats during an acute housing shortage. By the end of 1947, troops had already been used on five occasions as a strike-breaking force. The growing disillusion was indicated by Tom Harrisson's article in late 1947:

The British Institute of Public Opinion and *Daily Express* polls show a steady though slow quantitative decline in the popularity of the government and of the Prime Minister. But they do not show any corresponding increase in confidence in the Conservative Party or its leader.[14]

Likewise Mass-Observation in 1947 found that people are 'ready for radical action' but disappointed in the lack of 'spectacular appeals' and 'wider explanation' from the government.[15]

Neither did the fact of nationalization bring the feelings of identity and solidarity which the government had expected. A survey by the *Railway Review* at the end of 1948 showed that 48 per cent of the railwaymen who replied to a questionaire felt that their jobs were virtually unchanged, while another 45 per cent thought that frustration had increased after a year of nationaliz-ation. Fewer than 15 per cent of the respondents thought that they had a share in running the railways. A similar mood prevailed in the mines where the National Coal Board was as distant as, and acted no differently from, the old coal-owners. The *New Statesman* of 8 May 1948 summed up: 'The Board are remote from the ordinary worker, and the representatives of management with whom he comes into direct contact are nearly all the same per-sons as before.' Dissatisfaction flared up at the 1948 TUC Con-ference, and both the managers and trade union leaders confessed themselves puzzled by the frequent number of unofficial strikes: over 8,000 between 1947 and 1951. A series of studies on the nationalized industries by the Action Society, undertaken between 1950 and 1952, also reported the widespread feeling among the rank and file that public ownership had merely provided 'jobs for the boys', with 'the same old gang' in power again.

By 1948 the Labour government was clearly running out of steam and influential ministers like Herbert Morrison were call-ing for 'consolidation'.[16] But only now did the government em-bark upon its plan of nationalizing the iron and steel industry.

The bill put before the Commons in 1948 was cautious. The government envisaged an Iron and Steel Corporation which would own the assets and liabilities of the steel companies but undertake no change at all in their organizational and administrative structures.

The existing management and even the identities and names of the companies were to be retained intact. It was little more than a cosmetic exercise, but by 1948 business interests and industrialists felt confident enough to go on the offensive against the government—public relations firms like Aims of Industry were active, particularly in the 'Mr Cube' campaign opposing government plans for Tate and Lyle. The Steel Bill fell foul of the Tory majority in the House of Lords and thus the government found itself involved in a constitutional battle as well. The end result was the Parliament Act of 1949—not legislation abolishing the House of Lords or even hereditary peers, but rather curtailing to one year its power to delay bills passed by the House of Commons. The Iron and Steel Act did not come into operation until February 1951 because the government had agreed that the result of the 1950 election should be regarded as a mandate.

The potential remained. At the 1951 general election the Labour Party received just under 14 million votes, the highest that any party has ever received in this country, but the vagaries of the electoral system and the collapse of the Liberal Party vote returned a Conservative government. That so many votes were cast for the Attlee government underlines the point that in the space of six years many valuable reforms and changes had been introduced, and people were grateful for them. Health, social security and jobs were just three areas in which there had been enormous progress since the barren 1930s.

And yet…Throughout Jeremy Seabrook's *What Went Wrong?*, published in 1978, there is a persistent litany of disappointment voiced by elderly people recalling the hopes of 1945. As one speaker sadly observed: 'We had the opportunity in 1945. They had a thumping majority, they could have done anything with the people then.'[17]

Perhaps the answer lies in the constraints imposed by the worsening international situation, and in particular the heavy expenditure on armaments. Britain in the late 1940s was certainly no island but an integral part of what was now referred to as 'Western' Europe. Just how did such a division of Europe come about, and what were its consequences?

7. The making of Western Europe

The development of what is now called 'Western' Europe — although only since the late 1940s — is closely bound up with the United States, the country which emerged after the war as the most powerful in the world. Whereas following the 1914 – 18 war the USA had maintained a policy of isolationism, in the 1940s it embarked on a vigorous programme of international expansion. By 1950 there was not a single continent in which US business organizations were not influential or troops based.

The potential of the United States had become evident when, after the Civil War of the 1860s, industrialization occurred at a rapid pace, drawing upon the country's vast natural resources and pioneering such innovations as the assembly line. The population doubled between 1850 and 1900, providing supplies of cheap labour which were supplemented by the waves of immigrants coming across from Europe. Thus by 1914, to take just one crucial indicator, American steel output had overtaken those of both Britain and Germany.

The United States' marginal role in the First World War enhanced its strength as the European rivals battered themselves to pieces, and by the 1920s the American economy was clearly the most important in the world. The Great Crash of 1929 demonstrated the instabilities built into the capitalist system, but it also paradoxically threw American supremacy into greater relief by indicating how dependent the Europeans were on events the other side of the Atlantic. Roosevelt's New Deal with its relief and public works prodded the economy into growth once more although — a crucial pointer to the future — US recovery was confirmed only with the beginning of rearmament later in the 1930s.

During the Second World War the US economy expanded on a vast scale. Once again the country's rivals were destroying each other's factories, houses, schools and hospitals; in contrast, United States territory remained completely unscathed. In five years US industry increased by 40 per cent, corporate profits doubled to nearly 11 billion dollars, and the country's Gross National Product shot up by 60 per cent.

In addition, the system of Lend-Lease meant that America's allies had to pledge themselves to long-term sacrifices before receiving US aid; as Correlli Barnett has written of Britain:

Lend-Lease gradually consummated the process Churchill had begun of transforming England into an American satellite warrior-state dependent for its existence on the flow of supplies across the Atlantic. Indeed the very terms under which lend-Lease was operated both encouraged and emphasized the fact of her dependence. England had to agree not to sell articles abroad which contained Lend-Lease material, nor any goods, even if British-made, similar to goods received under Lend-Lease. An organization of American officials in England policed observance of these requirements, whose essential purpose was to ensure that British industry was switched wholly from exports to war production.[1]

On one hand other countries had to sell off their assets in continents such as Latin America. On the other, the United States' 'good neighbour' policy encouraged American domestic firms to move in on the newly vacated markets and huge organizations like General Motors, Standard Oil and ITT furthered their interests throughout the world. The US government also extended its influence in places such as the Pacific islands and, as with the gigantic corporations, these were not interests to be relinquished after the war.

By 1944, when the making of the postwar world was very much on the agenda, American business and politicians looked to have their dominance enshrined in future arrangements. At Bretton Woods in the summer of 1944, representatives of 44 nations met to discuss a new international monetary system. All the countries were supposed to enjoy equal status but in the circumstances this could not help but be illusory. The International Monetary Fund and later the World Bank, set up in 1946, were dominated by the USA. National currencies were tied to the dollar, the Federal Reserve was to be the world's central bank, and together with this went the 'open door' policy adopted unwillingly by 43 nations which ensured US penetration of their markets.

The death of President Roosevelt early in 1945 ushered in further changes. Roosevelt had always displayed certain humanitarian and internationalist attitudes which his successor Harry S. Truman signally lacked. As an example of Truman's primitive views there was his remark when the Nazis invaded the Soviet Union in the summer of 1941: 'If we see that Germany is winning the war we ought to help Russia, and if Russia is winning we ought to help Germany, and in that way let them kill as many as possible.' In particular, Truman viewed the world through two-dimensional glasses – 'them' and 'us'. Entries in his *Diary* indicate the reverse of Roosevelt's approach; for instance, he was fully aware of the extent of Soviet losses and devastation but his entry for August 1945 still reads: 'The Russians were planning world conquest.'[2]

Perhaps the most important decision in these years related to the development and control of the atomic bomb. Throughout the war Allied scientists had work on what was named the 'Tube Alloys Project', partly to pre-empt German research and partly to hasten the end of the conflict. From the start politicians shrouded the project in unnecessary secrecy – Churchill, for instance, omitted to tell the rest of the cabinet what was going on. The scientists, such as Niels Bohr, argued that the earth-shattering impact of this new weapon placed a responsibility on the American government to share control with the Allies. In 1945 scientists put forward proposals for exchanging such scientific information; their plan was vetoed by the American military heads.

In the summer of 1945 the horror of nuclear weapons was demonstrated at Hiroshima and Nagasaki. But, as the then Secretary of State, J.F.Byrnes, later acknowledged, the bomb was directed not so much against Japan but rather 'to make Russia manageable in Europe'.[3] With international control of nuclear weapons dismissed, the nuclear arms race was under way. By the end of the 1940s both Britain and the Soviet Union had their own bomb and the quest was now for a more powerful version.

American officials were surprised at the political developments obvious in Europe by the end of the war, especially at Churchill's defeat in the July 1945 election. Their response was quick: Lend-Lease to Britain was cancelled within days. In fact their alarm at the prospect of a labour government's foreign policy was mistaken. Ernest Bevin, the new Foreign Secretary, held thoroughly conventional views and he soon got over his ignorance of international affairs by instituting secret contacts with the Conservative shadow Foreign Minister, Anthony Eden.[4]

In France, too, a powerful figure was now in power whose aims were similar to those of the Truman administration. De Gaulle returned to France to October 1944 and significantly his first visits were paid to the Ministry of War and Police headquarters, not to the Committee of National Resistance. A conservative general was appointed as Minister of the Interior and lists of 'dependable' prefects drawn up.

Where possible de Gaulle hoped to establish traditional mechanisms of authority and General Eisenhower, the head of the Allied forces, has written of how de Gaulle: 'asked me for a temporary loan of two American divisions to use, as he said, as a show of force and to establish his position firmly.'[5] De Gaulle's worry was that the Resistance had left many of the people armed, but he managed to merge the patriotic militias into the regular armed forces and the local liberation committees were dissolved without a struggle.

A major reason for this ease of transistion lay in the strategy of the French Communist Party which, when its leader Maurice Thorez returned to the country, decided to don the mantle of respectability and lay low the bogey that it was not fit to govern. This meant that only strictly constitutional methods were to be followed.

The general election of October 1945 seemed to bring some form of pay-off as the French communists received more votes than any other party. In reality, however, they were being outmanoeuvered. There were five communists in de Gaulle's new government, with Thorez as vice-premier, but none of them held one of the key ministries of Foreign Affairs, Defence or the Interior. Together with this the compromises of government were now all too clear, as the communists found themselves discouraging strikes and wedded to a reactionary colonial policy. De Gaulle noted wonderingly in his memoirs: 'As for Thorez, even in his efforts to advance the communist cause, he will serve the national interest on a number of occasions. His constant call is for the maximum of work and production at any price. I shall not try to understand him. I am satisfied if France is served.'[6]

A similar chain of events was happening in Italy, with Togliatti playing the role of Thorez. At Salerno the Italian communists agreed to adopt a very broad approach, working on the basis of an anti-fascist coalition, dropping divisive socialist slogans and even postponing the question of the monarchy. In some ways this caution reflected the confused situation in Italy, with the Catholic Church an ever present force, a strong Allied army still there and the perennial split between the industrialized north and the rural south. Receiving four posts in Bonomi's administration from December 1944, the Italian communists also found themselves having to compromise – in this case supporting a wages freeze. After the elections of 1946 there were four communists in De Gasperi's coalition government.

In France, Italy, Britain, Belgium and elsewhere in Europe in the two years immediately following the war, important reforms and measures were introduced, clearing away much of the bitter legacy of the 1930s and the occupation: pensions, trade union rights, votes for women (in France and Italy in 1946, Belgium in 1948), public ownership of key industries and services, social insurance systems.

But the whole international atmosphere was changing, and this in turn had domestic consequences. In France the new elections of June 1946 saw a majority for the right-wing Democratic People's Movement, and in Italy Pope Pius XII moved on the attack, declaring in December 1946: 'Either with Christ or against Christ; either with his Church or against his Church.'[7] In November 1946 the Republicans had won a majority in the US Congress. So far the role of the American government had remained relatively low-key. Aid had been poured into Italy in an effort to take the sting out of the communists' demands and Lend-Lease with Britain had ceased, but there had been no direct attempts to intervene. But in 1947 the fragile European economy looked set to nose-dive again, and this time the Americans moved in on a permanent and massive scale.

The economic superiority of the USA meant that the ravaged European countries found themselves in no position to compete and were trading at a huge loss. 'Europe's deficits with the United States in 1946 and 1947 were, respectively, $4.2 billion and $5.4 billion.'[8] This was leading to a 'dollar shortage', and countries such as Italy – with over two-and-a-half million unemployed and inflation climbing rapidly – were experiencing severe difficulties. Similarly Britain was cutting back its commitments in India and also in Greece.

The preliminary American response came when President Truman asked Congress for a financial grant of $400 million in order to bolster the existing regimes in Greece and Turkey, proclaiming what came to be known as the 'Truman Doctrine': 'I believe that we must assist free peoples to work out their destiny in their own way.'

A few month later General Marshall, US Secretary of State, put forward plans for massive American assistance to Europe which were carried through as the European Recovery Programme. Later on, Marshall Aid was portrayed as a product of genuine idealism and selflessness, but this view conflicts with statements of the time. Marshall himself declared: 'It is idle to think that a Europe left to its own efforts…would remain open to American business in the same way that we have known it in the past.'[9] Truman later reflected: 'I think the world now realizes that without the Marshall Plan it would have been difficult for Western Europe to remain free from the tyranny of communism.'[10]

In other words, Marshall Aid was primarily motivated by American economic and political interests. The object was to block any radical change and maintain the position of US business by propping up right-wing regimes against the communist parties.

The first results were seen in the ousting of communist ministers. In May 1947 they were ejected from the French government which a few days later received a credit of $200 million. De Gasperi, the Italian Prime Minister, spent the beginning of 1947 in Washington and was advised to adopt a strong anti-communist posture; by June 1947 he felt sure enough to dismiss the communist ministers and was awarded a grant of $600 million. A similar chain of events occurred in Belgium. Again it was no coincidence that the respective governments all began to initiate some form of wage restraint.

Back in the United States the labour movement was also under attack. J.Edgar Hoover's FBI was actively at work in this area by 1947 and the Central Intelligence Agency (CIA) was set up the same year. The Taft-Hartley Act authorized the President to suspend strikes and in March 1947 Truman initiated a loyalty oath, an order which covered eight million people and their families. It did not matter a jot that of the six-and-a-half million people investigated between 1947 and 1952, not one example of espionage was discovered: it was the developing climate of fear and hysteria which counted.

In Europe it was the right-wing which benefited from such a mood. The Conservative Party in Britain was revitalized, and in France and Italy the newly-formed (with US aid) Catholic parties, the MRP and the Christian Democrats, emerged as the pivot of government. As Claude Julien has written:

> Conscious of its poor performance vis-à-vis fascism, the continental European Right found in anti-communism a road back to 'liberal' respectability, and seized the chance avidly. Beneath them, the middle classes were of course anxious to accede to the material prosperity of the American way of life.[11]

Professor Warner has pointed to the almost symmetrical character of events taking place in Europe at this time: 'If the presence of Soviet power was the major factor determining the postwar development of Eastern Europe, the presence of American power was no less important in determining that of the Western half of the continent.'[12]

It would not have been possible for attitudes in 'Western'

Europe to have changed so rapidly without the damaging activities of the communist parties. In the East there were the trials and purges, in the West the new communist organization the Cominform (Communist Information Bureau), set up in October 1947, prompted the Italian and French Communist Parties to launch a wave of strikes—thus seeming to bear out their description by conservatives as 'wreckers' of West European recovery.

Both the USA and the USSR cemented the other's hold over its own half of the continent, thereby destroying the 'Europe' which had emerged from the war. Valuable postwar reforms and measures had been instituted by the various governments, especially on welfare provision; but now superimposed were the priorities of the Cold War. And that meant enormous outlays on armaments expenditure, resources which both the West and the East could have spent more constructively.

8. The making of Eastern Europe

The Second World War had been fought out on the Eastern Front with a particular ferocity which rendered massacre and brutality the order of the day. One reason for this was that Nazi ideology regarded its neighbours to the east as sub-human; another lay in their plans to convert the area into 'food space' for the German people.

The end results were horrific. In Poland 8 million people, or 1 in 4 of the population, died; in Yugoslavia 2 million, or 1 in 9. The city of Warsaw alone, for example, had suffered more casualties than the United States and Britain combined.

Such devastation during the war aggravated the problems of a region of Europe that was in any case politically and economically backward. Many of the countries in central Europe and the Balkans, such as Bulgaria and Rumania, had emerged as 'succession states' after the Treaty of Versailles in 1919, and the various constitutions introduced in the early 1920s tried to establish a Western-style parliamentary democracy. But in every case hopes were at odds with reality.

The reality was one of meagre economic development with little industrialization. Communications were poor, with Albania, for instance, having no railway whatever. Agriculture remained primitive with barely any mechanization and wooden ploughs still in widespread use, the land farmed in too-small units by too many people. There were few hospitals or schools, and illiteracy and superstition flourished.

The lack of industry and an educated middle class meant that there was no tradition of parliamentary democracy and in every country, except Czechoslovakia, authoritarian regimes were established. During the 1930s the Germans extended their influence in the region, propping up the various dictators and encouraging the growth of fascist parties—just as in the nineteenth century it had been the Russians and the Austrians who had treated the countries as their own colonies.

Then came the war which, although it caused the downfall of many of these oppressive regimes, exacerbated an already difficult state of affairs. Matters were confused further by the 'great power' arrangements whereby areas of influence and control were laid down, and by the varying strength of the Resistance movements. For example, in Yugoslavia there were 800,000 Partisans, broadly based and with a recognized leader in Tito, but in Hungary virtually none. Finally the formidable Red army remained—the force which had been responsible for the installation of the new governments barring that of Bulgaria.

Although the Soviet Union was undoubtedly the strongest power in this part of Europe, it is worth recalling the consequences of the war. The German invasion in 1941 was the second time in 25 years that the country found itself occupied in large part by enemy forces; by 1945 the Soviet Union had been wrecked:

> The economy was near collapse. At least a quarter of all
> Soviet property had been destroyed. Nearly 2,000 towns
> and 70,000 villages had been razed, and 25 million people
> were homeless. Soviet industry had achieved a prodigious
> output of tanks, guns, aircraft, and other materials, but this
> obscured the fact that industry as a whole had suffered
> disastrously. Some 31,000 factories, including the major
> industries in Kharkov, Krivoi Rog, Zaporozhie, Rostov,
> Odessa, Leningrad and Stalingrad had been destroyed.[1]

The Soviet Union was still a great power, but the United States possessed far more resources.

In view of such Soviet destruction, Stalin's main concern in 1945 was 'never again!' The USSR must be sure that neighbouring countries were friendly—unlike the 1930s when they were hostile. Governments in Bulgaria, Rumania and Hungary all supported the German invasion of June 1941. The Soviet Union had suffered huge losses in clearing the various countries of the Nazis: 300,000 troops were killed in Poland alone.

The USSR's concern with security was widely understood. A study by the Chatham House Study Group in 1946, whose members included a clutch of generals and admirals, read:

> The Russian view of Eastern Europe as a zone in which she is vitally concerned for reasons of national security and in which, therefore, her voice should carry the greatest weight, arouses no opposition in Britain and it is understood that, after her experiences in the war, Russia is naturally 'security-conscious'. Nor does it seem unreasonable that she should wish the governments of neighbouring countries to be well-disposed towards her.[2]

Of course Soviet fears were augmented by the knowledge that the United States had a monopoly on the atom bomb.

At first, however, in the comparatively friendly international situation of the mid-1940s, there was little need for concern on the Soviet side. The impetus of the war had led to the downfall of the various reactionary regimes and their replacement by anti-fascist coalitions in which the well-organized communists played an important but not a dominating role. In every country similar policies were pursued in an attempt to avoid a return to the destitution of the interwar years. These revolved around two tasks: the need to break up the old semi-feudal landowners' estates and thus redistribute the land, and to stimulate the development of industrialization. The first was carried out by means of large-scale land reforms, the second through sweeping nationalization. They effectively ended the 'old order'.

The extent of the land reforms can be gauged by the huge areas redistributed. In Hungary the agrarian reform law of March 1945 authorized one-third of the cultivated fields to be divided amongst half-a-million peasants. In Poland six million hectares were redistributed, and in Rumania two million acres. Longstanding peasant debts were also cancelled and co-operative enterprises introduced. Paradoxically, although the land was now shared out on a more equitable basis, the fragmentation that this entailed was no encouragement to agricultural efficiency because the peasant smallholders lacked the capital to mechanize their methods. Collective farms were alien to the fierce individualism of the peasants and matters were worsened by the poor harvests of 1946 and 1947.

As for industrialization, the problems in the past had centred around the paucity of domestic investment and the dominance of foreign capital, crippling each country with debts. Furthermore the few industrialists there were had invariably collaborated with the Germans.

One of the first actions therefore of the coalition governments was to confiscate the property of all collaborators and war criminals, and in a country like Yugoslavia this resulted in over 80 per cent of her industry passing into state control. But elsewhere such measures were inadequate and the governments embarked on a programme of massive public ownership. In Czechoslovakia 2,000 firms were taken over from October 1945; in Hungary banking, mines, electricity and heavy industry had all been nationalized by November 1947; and in Bulgaria by the end of 1947 over 6,000 concerns were in public ownership.

National economic plans were drawn up, setting out targets to be reached and co-ordinating the various enterprises so that they would dovetail with, and not compete against, each other. Together with this went the tremendous energy unleashed by the war, ensuring that such programmes were generally successful. The historian Roy Medvedev has written of the Soviet Union: 'After the war, industrial growth rates rose sharply. As early as 1947 most indices were back to prewar levels or above them. The country's great moral and political exaltation had a marked effect on the development of the national economy.'[3]

Nor was this process restricted to the Soviet Union. Neal Ascherson has written of Poland that

Reconstruction, including the rebuilding of Warsaw, went ahead with a speed and energy which astonished the outside world. Living standards began to recover, and real wages rose above their prewar levels. And the fundamental transformation of Polish society took its first decisive steps as rapid industrialization began to draw people off the appallingly overcrowded countryside.[4]

Both land reform and public ownership enjoyed much popular support. The various coalition governments seemed to be tackling difficulties and obstacles in broadly similar ways which did, however, allow some leeway for specific national characteristics. This caution was necessary because in some countries, most notably Poland, institutions such as the Catholic Church were the most influential and even the USSR had fought the 1941−5 conflict as a 'great patriotic war' and not as a European civil war.

The Soviet Union was at this time extracting sizeable reparations from its neighbours. At least 2,000 million dollars worth of resources were removed from Rumania in 1944 alone; East Germany paid $15,800 million between 1945 and 1953[5]; and a series of joint-stock companies was established on terms highly favourable to the Soviet economy. A unanimity of foreign policy was also required, but apart from that (admittedly a big 'that') the governments within the Soviet 'sphere of influence' were permitted to implement domestic policies drawn up by themselves.

But nowhere could stand outside the increasingly bitter international situation. Europe was starting to polarize, and Marshall Aid in 1947 led to an extension of American influence in 'Western' Europe. To the east, so too did the communist parties began to increase their power. Within the coalition governments they had often provided the drive behind the economic reforms and invariably occupied the key ministries of Defence, Foreign Affairs and the Interior, ideally placed to oust non-communist colleagues.

The coalition administrations all began to disintegrate at about the same time. In Poland, Rumania and Bulgaria during the autumn of 1947 the three non-communist leaders−Mikolajczk, Maniu and Petkov−were either forced to leave the country or put on trial for treason. In Hungary the security police conveniently uncovered a fascist plot in May 1947 and the opposition Smallholders Party was destroyed. The transition in Czechoslovakia came later, in February 1948, when the question of the control of the police led the non-communist ministers to resign en bloc. In every case the communists came to power contrary to the Yalta Conference which had promised 'free and unfettered elections...on the basis of universal suffrage and secret ballot'.

With communists ejected from governments in the west, and non-communists in the east, Europe was being divided into two rival and opposing sides. Just as Pope Pius XII announced that one was either for or against the Church, so did Zhdanov the Soviet leader proclaim his 'two camp' doctrine, 'us or them', 'for or against' 'one way or the other'.

The two overseers were tightening their reins and the room for manoeuvre decreased. Both the Czech and Polish governments were initially in favour of accepting an invitation to the preliminary conference in Paris on the Marshall Plan in July 1947, but Soviet pressure brought a reversal. 'National' roads to socialism were dismissed and in September 1947 the Cominform, seeking to impose the Soviet model of development, decreed that the various governments should now move towards the collectivization of agriculture — this despite the knowledge that it would destroy popular support for the new postwar regimes as well as bring repression in its wake as the peasants fought against the measure. Stalin had remarked to Churchill at Yalta that such a programme in the Soviet Union had been a more perilous undertaking even than the Battle of Stalingrad.

Only one country within the boundaries of Soviet influence rebelled against this regimentation — Yugoslavia. The self-confidence of the Partisan movement, inspired by its size and victories against the Germans, had enabled Tito to secure the concession from Stalin that the Red army would possess no administrative or civil powers in Yugoslavia. This was a portent of things to come.

After the war the Yugoslav government adopted similar policies to those elsewhere. The Constituent Assembly elected in the autumn of 1945 abolished the monarchy and sanctioned land reform and nationalization. The distribution of land gave rise to the usual drawback. With 12 million peasants sharing 20 million acres of arable land, this meant less than two acres a person. But in one respect the Yugoslavs were already different. Tito refused to sanction joint-stock companies with the Soviet Union whereby, as in the other countries, materials and resources were siphoned off to the latter. At first, in the liberal atmosphere prevailing after the war, Yugoslav actions were an irritant but no more to Moscow. But by 1948 and the era of the two camps, matters came to a head.

Early in 1948 trade talks between the Soviet Union and Yugoslavia broke down. Soviet advisers were withdrawn from the country and in June 1948 a Cominform communiqué roundly condemned and expelled Yugoslavia from the organization. Yugoslavia was to be thrown out of the communist fold. It is worth noting that the only other communist European country which later broke with the Soviet Union – Albania – also had a very strong Resistance movement during the war.

The Yugoslav breach heralded an onslaught against all those whom Moscow suspected of being 'national deviationists' – that is, did not think the Soviet system could be applied lock, stock and barrel to their own countries. In the context of the one-party state – the monopoly of power by respective communist parties and the elimination of all opposition – this led to a wave of trials and purges. One recent historian has written of 'the ease with which prominent party officials – using their links with security forces – could crush any criticism from within the party and eliminate people who, on grounds of background or even some personal characteristic, they happened to dislike.'[6] In Poland Gomulka and six other ministers were stripped of their posts and imprisoned. In Bulgaria 10 out of 16 communist ministers and six out of nine members of the politbureau lost their jobs. In Hungary Laszlo Rajk, the leader of the Hungarian underground during the war and then Minister of the Interior, was hanged in 1949. Nor was it only the leaders who suffered; many ordinary party members met secret execution and thousands were expelled from the Communist Party and thus lost their jobs.

> Between September and December 1948, 30,000 members were expelled from the Polish Communist Party. In August 1948, 100,000 were expelled from the Czechoslovak Party and half a million were reduced from full to candidate membership. In 1949–50, 92,500 members were expelled from the Bulgarian Party. About two-and-a-half million people were purged in all between 1948 and 1952, and of these between 125,000 and 250,000 were imprisoned.[7]

The fate of one man must stand for thousands. Traicho Kostov was a veteran Bulgarian communist who for 30 years had devoted himself to the labour movement, and after the war was appointed deputy prime minister. In November 1949 he was arrested and tried for conspiring with Tito to do all manner of things; in addition Kostov was damningly accused of having had Trotskyite sympathies. The show trial began and, quite unexpectedly, Kostov suddenly retracted the 'confessions' he had made whilst in prison. He insisted throughout the trial that he was innocent, but to no avail: Kostov was sentenced to death and executed. Conveniently the press published a letter after his death 'by' Kostov in which he owned up to everything. The Bulgarian leadership subsequently sent a telegram to Beria, Stalin's police chief: 'Only your deeply penetrating eye could see in time the criminal spy gang of Kostov.'[8] In 1956 it was revealed by the Bulgarian authorities that everything to do with Kostov's trial and execution had been fabricated.

From 1949 it is possible to talk of 'Eastern Europe' as a more or less monolithic block. 'Comecon' was founded in order to assist economic integration and in some cases this process of uniformity was accelerated by various countries' dependence on Soviet raw materials. For example, Poland's textiles needed cotton from Soviet Central Asia, its iron and steel ore came from the Eastern Ukraine and its oil from the Caucasus. In all the countries, and in response to the growing armaments race, governments stressed heavy industry at the expense of consumer goods and social services. About 25 per cent of the national income was to be reinvested in heavy industry. The Communist Party controlled all levels of society, trade unions were taken over and labour regulation introduced in an attempt to promote rapid economic growth.

It is dangerous to make glib generalizations about Eastern Europe in the 1940s. On the one hand civil rights were ignored and abused. Elections had become a farce; in Bulgaria, for example, the Fatherland Front received 98 per cent of the votes for the National Assembly in December 1949 and even a sympathetic observer wrote: 'the vote was too high in a country of admitted shortage to carry complete conviction.'[9] The gap between the party and the people was demonstrated by 'the cult of personality' which grew up, particularly around Stalin himself.

On the other hand, backward countries had been transformed. The numbers receiving secondary and higher education more than doubled, facilities for the young and women, the old and the sick were introduced, and the standard of living rose by leaps and bounds. One woman, whose husband had perished in a Czech show trial of 1952 and was thus unlikely to exaggerate the benefits, wrote of her life in the early 1950s with villagers in rural Czechoslovakia who were predominantly Catholic:

> Although they would often grumble at the difficulties of everyday life, socialism had brought secure employment to these upland parts, where it was hard to win a living by farming alone, the husbands of many held good jobs in nearby towns, their children could study at secondary schools, not a few went on to universities, the generous social insurance system was a boon, and no one, except perhaps some former people of property, was anxious to see the old prewar days come back.[10]

But the major factor bearing down on the postwar development of this whole area — and the reason why 'Eastern' Europe itself came into existence — was the Cold War.

9. The Cold War

The phrase 'the Cold War' is one in common usage, especially today, describing the hostility between the United States and the Soviet Union. It is often thought of as a product of the Second World War and after. In fact one needs to go back to 1917 in order to understand attitudes towards the USSR

When the Bolsheviks seized power during the October Revolution they did so with an ideology which directly challenged the rest of the world. Their actions matched their words. Lenin's government repudiated the country's past debts, exposed the system of prewar secret diplomacy and pulled out of the war. Industries were nationalized and landholdings split up in order to satisfy the peasants. The response of the former allies was immediate — a 'crusade' of 14 nations to overthrow this new and independent regime, with troops and aid supplied by, amongst others, Britain, France and the United States.

This Russian Civil War ended in 1920, the Bolsheviks remaining in control of a now thoroughly ravaged country. However the enmity continued, although Stalin's policy of 'socialism in one country' lessened the antagonism from the late 1920s, as did the USSR joining the League of Nations in 1934. The Nazi — Soviet Pact of 1939 brought about renewed abuse of the Soviet Union, a position reversed in 1941 when the Germans invaded.

As the war drew to a close both the Americans and the Soviets were anxious to install 'satisfactory' regimes in the countries they occupied. Stalin put it succinctly in a speech of July 1944: 'This war is not as in the past; whoever occupies a territory also imposes on it his own social system. Everyone imposes his own systems as far as his army can reach. It cannot be otherwise.'[1]

The tension really came when and where the Allied and Soviet forces confronted each other directly, and it was Germany which was the major issue at the heart of the Cold War.

After defeat in the First World War and the upheaval of the 1920s with massive inflation and unemployment, stability ensued only when Germany was recognized and supported as a bulwark against the Soviet Union. Industrialists financed Hitler from the early 1930s as an additional safety measure, knowing full well that his policies entailed the destruction of the labour movement and increased their profits.[2]

For the rest of the population Nazism brought less tangible rewards and the war itself led to severe deprivation. By 1945 Germany had been devastated, as people can see today by watching Roberto Rossellini's film *Germany: Year Zero*. An English visitor wrote of Hamburg: 'An area the size of Birmingham had been razed to the ground, suburb after suburb had been wiped out.'[3] As late as January 1947 an English theatre company toured Berlin: 'It was difficult to find streets. There were just neat piles of rubble.'[4]

The country itself had been split into four zones, each of them occupied by one of the victorious powers – the Soviet Union, the USA, Britain and France. Berlin, in the middle of the Soviet zone, was the headquarters of the Allied Control Council. The main question centred on the prospects and character of the future Germany and this whole issue was discussed most fully at the Potsdam Conference in the summer of 1945.

The Potsdam Agreement of 2 August 1945 was quite clear on the need to root out German militarism and Nazism and 'to prepare for the eventual reconstruction of German political life on a democratic basis and for eventual peaceful co-operation in international life by Germany.' The agreement went on to call for the elimination or control of all German industry that could be used for military production, and the ending of 'the present excessive concentration of economic power as exemplified by cartels, trusts and other monopoly associations'.

This envisaged far-reaching economic and social changes, the construction of a new and very different order along the lines of Hungary or Yugoslavia with land reforms, the nationalization of heavy industry, extensive 'denazification' and the payment of reparations. And in the Soviet zone such action soon followed, with seven million acres of land confiscated during September 1945 and then redistributed, and a central plan drawn up for industrial growth. Finally in the Soviet zone, all the key jobs in the trade unions and administration were held by people with a background of anti-Nazi activity, with over 260 Denazification Committees combing through the histories of important officials.

In the Western zones progress was much slower. US officials were not happy with the idea of sweeping social reforms, and it was becoming clearer by the day just what such changes entailed in the countries to the east. Thus by 1946 the idea of a separate state — the division of Germany — was already being canvassed. The American government was increasingly asking itself whether it might not be better to create a separate West German state within their sphere of influence rather than risk losing all — a united Germany subject to the same policies and pressures as its Eastern neighbours.

Leaders of the right-wing Christian Democrats like Konrad Adenauer were of the same mind. Another was Erich Kohler who stated quite categorically: 'We reject the unity of Germany if the socialist forces were thereby able to rule over the whole Germany.' General Lucius Clay, the head of military government in the US zone up to 1949, writes in his book *Decision in Germany* that he had already decided by May 1946 to approach the British about unifying their respective zones — the next step towards the division of Germany. The growing polarization was summed up by Winston Churchill in his famous speech at Fulton, Missouri in March 1946: 'From Stettin in the Baltic to Trieste in the Adriatic an iron curtain has descended across the continent.'

The programme of land reform and public ownership in the 'Western' zones slithered to a halt, and on the two vital issues of the destruction of cartels and monopolies and the task of denazification the policy went into reverse. Regarding the first question James S. Martin, chief of the decartelization branch of the US military government, resigned in 1947 in protest against the half-hearted implementation of the Potsdam agreement: 'The effect in Germany was the same as if the original architects of the new order (the Nazis) had been in charge.'[5]

As for denazificaiton, the Americans found that if their zones were to be restored to what they regarded as economic health then it meant relying on past Nazi members and sympathizers. For example, the US weekly *Saturday Evening Post* wrote about the steel trust in October 1946: 'To be precise, of the 361 top executives who were members of the Nazi party only 33 have been arrested. All others are still in their old jobs.' Alfred Krupp, the head of the largest Nazi arms organization, was originally sentenced to 12 years' imprisonment and the confiscation of his property by a US court; within three years he was back at the head of the trust. The US denazification chief, Joseph Napoli, declared in 1949 that denazification in the US zone had gradually degenerated into the whitewashing of Nazis.

But the most notorious example of the failure of denazification is provided by the career of Klaus Barbie, the 'Butcher of Lyons'. Barbie had been responsible for the torture and death of many members of the French Resistance druing the war, and by 1946 he was being sought by both British and US intelligence services. However, in 1947 Barbie was recruited by US counter-intelligence officers when he offered them information about communists who had fought in the Resistance. In 1949 the French demanded Barbie's extradition, but the next year he escaped with American help to Bolivia.[6]

Throughout 1947 relations between the United States and the Soviet Union continued to deteriorate. The British and Americans, who had already economically amalgamated their zones, fused them totally in late 1947 forming 'Bizonia'. A part of the friction centred on the currency arrangements, with the Reichsmark providing one of the few remaining links between the four zones. In June 1948, after secret preparations, the Western Block introduced the new currency of the 'Deutschmark'. The Russians regarded this as the final straw and responded with a blockade of West Berlin; the Americans proceeded to airlift supplies in until the blockade was lifted in May 1949. The Cold War had arrived with a vengeance.

Events after that merely confirmed the division of Germany, and hence of Europe, into two antagonistic blocks. On the American side a parliamentary council was constituted under Dr Konrad Adenauer to draft a West German constitution, their results – the 'Basic Law' – being adopted in May 1949. The new state was proclaimed on 7 September 1949 with Bonn as its capital and a week later Dr Adenauer as its Chancellor. With 'West' Germany in existence, 'East' Germany was not long in following: the German Democratic Republic was founded in October 1949.

The Cold War had a number of crucially important consequences. It split organizations such as the United Nations and the World Federation of Trade Unions: prompted the growth of a whole range of bodies which flourished in these conditions; poisoned the political, social and cultural atmosphere; and significantly, fuelled the arms race.

The United Nations had been founded in June 1945, and Article 1 spoke of safeguarding world peace, protecting human rights, ensuring equal rights for all peoples and improving living standards throughout the world. But before long the use of the veto was a commonplace, with the USA and USSR glowering at each other across the table. Similarly the World Federation of Trade Unions, established in 1945, was polarized by the Marshall Plan and in 1949 the 'West' left to set up the International Confederation of Free Trade Unions with US aid.[7]

The late 1940s also saw the development of a number of organizations which by their very existence had a stake in the continuation of the Cold War. In Britain there was the Information Research Department (IRD), a bland name for a body specializing in anti-communist material. Established in 1947 by members of the Labour government, it circulated documents to the cabinet, MPs and journalists as well as to contacts abroad. By 1951 the IRD was publishing more than 1,000 articles a year to be distributed by the Foreign Office all over the world – and financed by the 'secret vote', the money allocated to the secret services over which parliament exercises no supervision. In fact IRD's existence was not made known to MPs until the 1970s.[8]

In West Germany Axel Springer, who began his career in 1946 with a sports magazine, acquired a whole range of newspapers and periodicals; the political line of Springer's publications being an unrelenting anti-communism. West Germany was, and still is, the location of the American-financed Radio Free Europe and Voice of America, born in the Cold War and staffed by East European emigrés. US money was also channelled into organizations like the Congress for Cultural Freedom, founded in Berlin in 1950 and later responsible for the right-wing magazine *Encounter*, and also from 1950s, the International Student Conference—an anti-communist front.

American aid helped to create a number of political parties and trade unions. The Christian Democrats in Italy received a $1 million grant and De Gaulle's new party founded in 1947 was also helped out. The Force Ouvrière was assisted in breaking away from the largest French trade union, the CGT, and the division of the Italian General Confederation of Labour was financed by the US. Both the French and Italian socialist parties were encouraged to keep their distance from their respective communist parties.[9]

In such a context it is not surprising that it was the conservative parties who enjoyed almost uninterrupted success throughout Western Europe. The Conservatives in Britain returned to office in 1951 and remained for the next 13 years. The Christian Democrats in Italy have been in power ever since 1948 and in France, although individual socialists have been members of administrations, the right wing controlled the levers of power until the success of Mitterrand. Within the various labour parties themselves it was once again the right-wing—untainted by any association with 'the left' and hence 'communism'—who predominated. In the British Labour Party of the 1950s the 'revisionism' of men like Anthony Crosland and Hugh Gaitskell was powerful; and the West German Social Democrats had by the end of that decade dropped their socialist programmes.

In Eastern Europe opposition had been ruthlessly eliminated; the Communist Party exercised a stranglehold on power and the trade unions did not exist as independent bodies. The security apparatus was expanded and in Poland, for instance, the Security Office instituted a secret Tenth Department in 1952 which kept an eye on the Communist Party itself. In the Soviet Union Beria remained in charge of the secret police and the bloodletting continued. In 1949–50 there was the Leningrad Affair, an opportunity for rivals within the party hierarchy to pay off old scores by means of the firing squad.

With accusation and abuse the order of the day, the rhetoric on both sides took on an increasingly shrill tone. T.S.Eliot inveighed against 'barbarian nomads', and even Harold Macmillan could be found warning of 'the invasion of the Goths' and calling for a Christian Crusade.[10] The vetting of civil servants for their political views was instigated in 1948, and the smear of 'communist plot' was used to refer to any legitimate trade dispute — such as the strike at the London docks in 1949.[11] Techniques like these were later to be used widely in the USA by Senator Joe McCarthy.

Hollywood produced films with lurid titles such as *I Married a Communist*, *I was a Communist for the FBI* and *The Red Menace*. Books like *The God that Failed*, published in 1950, paraded disillusioned ex-communists who now assailed their former 'faith', and George Orwell's *1984* and Arthur Koestler's *Darkness at Noon* chimed in with this mood, whatever their authors' intentions might have been.

In Eastern Europe the search was for 'Titoites' or the familiar 'Trotskyites'. Soviet culture and learning were thoroughly 'purified' by Zhdanov. 'The Zhdanovskchina (Zhdanov's purge) when it came in 1948—9 was extremely thorough and wide-ranging — little less than an intellectual terror, launched against all institutions of creativity, criticism and higher education.'[12] Elsewhere it was a similar story. The Writers' Union in Poland was purged in 1950 and the orthodoxy of 'socialist realism' imposed.

For the 'ordinary' people of Europe the sense of being trapped between two immovable objects was overwhelming. Mass-Observation reported on the apathy and scepticism which this was causing in Britain. 'The overall impression is one of increasing resignation to the idea of another war, less expression of indignation, a more fatalistic attitude, now that the atom bomb had become more familiar.'[13]

Only one country, Yugoslavia, was perched between the East—West divide, and the achievements there in the postwar world provide some indication of what could have been done without the polarizing effects of the Cold War. The system of federal government had welded together this disparate region and its nation-alities, which just a few years before had been at each other's throats. The land and public ownership reforms resulted in a greatly increased standard of living, and in the early 1950s the practice of self-management was pioneered with workers' councils elected by secret ballot every two years. The forced crops delivery was stopped in 1952 — in contrast to elsewhere in Eastern Europe. The Communist Party retained its pivotal position but the Federal and Communal Councils were elected by means of universal suffrage. It would be wrong to overglamorize — the secret police retained considerable power — but the country did exemplify the concrete realization of some of the wartime hopes and aspirations.[14]

But the most important consequence of the Cold War was the ever-growing arms race, a development which undermined many programmes of social reform and still haunts us today. For in-stance Britain maintained throughout the late 1940s armed forces at a figure three times their 1939 size, and the average military expenditure each year by the Labour government was about £750 million, or over 10 per cent of the national income. In 1947 there were still over one million men and women in the services, whilst at the same time the *Economic Survey* of February 1947 was report-ing that Britain faced severe difficulties because of a chronic labour shortage of 600,000 people.

Most of the American aid to Western Europe was swallowed up in increased military expenditure. For example France received 875 milliard francs between 1948 and 1951 under the Marshall Plan; in the same years it spent 1,950 milliard francs on arms. In 1949 the United States exported military goods worth 506 million dollars; this was ten times the pre-1939 value of armaments trading between all countries. In the Soviet Union resources were diverted away from the Fourth Five-Year Plan, adopted in 1946, towards military expenditure and particularly the search for their own atom bomb.

Looking back now, one is struck by the climate of fear and hysteria with which the whole question of the 'communist threat' was discussed. The *Times* of 15 June 1981 carried a report that the chiefs of staffs in 1946 had been studying a plan for an attack on Russian cities with more than 100,000 inhabitants, using atomic bombs and germ warfare. Again, in the summer of 1951 Whitehall's Joint Intelligence Committee is to be found discussing ways and means of preventing the Red army from crossing the North Sea and the Channel.[15]

Plans for integrating the military efforts of Western Europe with those of the United States continued apace. In the summer of 1948 American military bases were established in Britain, and in April 1949 the pact setting up the North Atlantic Treaty Organization (NATO) was signed in Washington. In the same month the Soviet government put forward proposals for the unification of Germany, which were rejected. John Foster Dulles, the Republican Party's foreign affairs expert and later Secretary of State, explained why: 'The reason was that some feared any relaxation of the East–West tension would bring a corresponding relaxation on the part of the American people and therefore they needed to be kept artificially alarmed.'[16]

The anxieties of the American government were exacerbated by the victory of Mao Tse-Tung's forces over the US-backed Chiang Kai-Shek dictatorship and the creation of the Chinese People's Republic in October 1949. By now Europe and the rest of the world was strictly partitioned into 'them' and 'us'. In this powder-keg situation, the outbreak of the Korean War in June 1950 hardened the division.

Korea itself provided a mirror image of Europe, split between the North, which was communist-supported, and the South, where the Americans had installed Premier Syngman Rhee. The 38th Parallel formed the border, and eventually a series of disputes and limited invasions erupted into civil war. Fought with great brutality, over two million Koreans lost their lives. The Chinese were sucked in on the North Korean side and American generals advocated use of the atomic bomb, but the war was finally concluded by an armistice in 1953. The frontier was fixed where it had begun: at the 38th Parallel.

The importance of the Korean War lay in the way in which it reinforced and cemented the international polarization; as Elisabeth Barker has written: 'Within six months it had turned the Atlantic Alliance from a paper document into an integrated defence system under an American supreme commander, with the West

Europeans embarking on impossibly ambitious rearmament programmes.'[17]

By the early 1950s an iron curtain did indeed separate Eastern and Western Europe, just as it divided Germany into East and West. The optimism and vision of the early 1940s were not even a distant memory.

10. Forty years on

Where did the Forties go? In large part they were dissipated by subsequent events – particularly the Cold War – and the power of these events has been such that they have effectively wiped out much of what went before. To go back to the early and mid-1940s calls for a tremendous leap of the imagination because certain attitudes which today are dismissed or ignored were then common-sensical and almost taken for granted.

Return to, say, 1943 when Sir William Beveridge told a meeting at Caxton Hall in London:

> My Report as a whole is intended to give effect to what I regard as a peculiarly British idea: the idea of a national minimum wage, which we learnt from the trade unions and have embodied in Trade Board acts, is necessary but isn't sufficient. There is wanted also a minimum income for subsistence when wages fail for any reason; a minimum of provision for children; a minimum of health, of housing, of education.[1]

The assumption made in this speech – that the entitlement of everyone to a minimum standard to living is a priority – now appears old-fashioned. In present-day Britain, where the whole consensus which emerged from the war is under attack – the welfare state, full employment and a public sector – it would be foolish to make such an assumption.

In a number of ways the 1940s still cast a lengthy shadow. Take, for example, the whole question of public ownership. During the war, as we saw, many institutions and services which had been privately run in peacetime for the sake of private profit had simply broken down under wartime conditions. Transport, fuel, housing, health, education, welfare, even the distribution of food—were all popularly regarded from early on during the war as areas which, if they were to be run efficiently and fairly, needed to be administered in large part by the government and local authorities. Now, however, 'nationalization' is a bogey word and 'privatization' all the rage, with public assets being sold off to the highest bidder and the welfare state and nationalized industries starved of resources.

The 1940s are also a period over which memories and inter-pretations conflict; it is here that historians, civil servants, politicians and journalists fight out a never-ending battle. In America during the 1950s, orthodoxy held that it was the Russians who had been bent on conquest and aggression after the war. In the 1960s, the 'revisionist' school arose which emphasized the role of the United States in fomenting the Cold War. Now, with the onset of the new Cold War, the pendulum is swinging back again—and a similar process has also occurred in the Soviet Union. There the 'revisionism' sparked off by Khrushchev in 1956 led to a more critical examination of Stalin's policies and behaviour. This liberalizing trend seems to have lasted only a few years or so, the removal of Khrushchev in 1964 signalling the beginning of a more rigorous censorship. The Soviet historian Alexander Nekrich wrote in *Index on Censorship*, in August 1980 that 'It is impossible to research the problems of genocide in the USSR, Soviet—German relations in the Hitler period, and particularly the problems of their collaboration in 1939—41.'

In Britain censorship is rather more subtle and indirect, Whitehall's 'weeders' trawling the records and destroying sensitive material prior to public access. The affairs of the Information Research Department, noted in the last chapter, will perforce remain secret because the documents relating to that department have been shredded. The *Observer* for 28 February 1982 related the answer of the Lord Chancellor's department when questioned about this vandalism: 'The items...distributed by IRD to other FO [Foreign Office] departments and journalists were in the main ephemeral and not considered to be of sufficient historical importance to be selected for permanent preservation.' The people doing the considering, and the criteria themselves, are, of course, 'classified'. One more example from the 1940s: the historian of 'denazification', Tom Bower, has written that 'The British have destroyed most of their archives on the occupation of Germany, a convenient excuse to conceal their own unsavoury dealings.'[2]

The tramlines laid down in the late 1940s have had not just political but also social and economic consequences, arising in particular from the arms race prompted by the Cold War. One indication of the growth of military spending is that between 1945 and 1980 armaments expenditure actually quadrupled in size in real terms. Today well over a million dollars a minute are spent on weapons, and the introduction of nuclear weapons has led to a frantic search for bigger and better methods of destruction.

This proliferation of nuclear arms within the Cold War context means that, even leaving aside the intentions of both superpowers, the chances of an accidental holocaust have risen enormously. A document published in December 1980 by the US Defence Department revealed that there had been 27 serious nuclear accidents in the United States since the war. In January 1961, for instance, an aircraft jettisoned two nuclear bombs over North Carolina. One bomb was caught in a tree and the jolting released five of its six safety switches. Only one switch prevented the explosion of a 24 megaton bomb, 1,800 times more powerful than the bomb dropped on Hiroshima in 1945.[3] Nor has Britain been immune from such near-disasters. A B-47 bomber crashed at Lakenheath in July 1956 and its three nuclear bombs were in immediate danger of being ignited by blazing fuel. In which case, one US airforce general considered, 'it is possible that a part of eastern England would have become a desert.'[4]

At present some $600,000,000,000 is spent annually worldwide on military budgets. Within EEC countries themselves, Britain laid out $24.4 billion in 1980, West Germany $25.1 billion and France $20.2 billion. All these figures have risen since then, and the advent of Cruise and Pershing missiles, plus in Britain the cost of Trident, will send them spiralling further upwards.[5]

Yet at the same time the standard of living for many within the EEC is falling. An EEC report issued in December 1981 found that 30 million people within the Community existed in poverty, and this figure will have been aggravated by the rise in unemployment. More than a quarter of Europe's young people are now without a job. Within Britain, the government's own statistics show that between November 1979 and March 1983 the number of people dependent on supplementary benefit rose from 4.3 million to 7 million, one in eight of the population. The *Breadline Britain* series broadcast by London Weekend Television during summer 1983, estimated that 7.5 million people in Britain are living in poverty, with three-quarters of a million in intense poverty. The most vulnerable groups are single-parent families, the unemployed, the elderly, the disabled and sick, and the low-paid—all the people for whom Sir William Beveridge in the 1940s had proposed a minimum of provision.

The Cold War division established in the 1940s, splitting up Europe and much of the world into rival 'sphere of influence', has become a fact of life. The US and USSR act like adversaries on opposite sides of a ring; threatening or repressive actions from one side invariably trigger off a similar response from the other. In 1955 West Germany was rearmed and allowed full membership of NATO, and the Soviet reaction was to set up the Warsaw Pact—six years after NATO.

Similarly the British and French invasion of Egypt the next year, set off by Nasser's nationalization of the Suez Canal, helped the Soviet Union when it sent troops into Hungary later that year. Veljko Micunovic, the Yugoslav ambassador to Moscow at the time, records how this process worked:

Khrushchev said that British and French aggressive
pressure on Egypt provided a favourable moment for further
intervention by Soviet troops. It would help the Russians.
There would be confusion and uproar in the West and the
United Nations, but it would be less at a time when Bri-
tain, France and Israel were waging a war against Egypt.
'They are bogged down there, and we are stuck in
Hungary,' Khrushchev said.[6]

Others made the same connection: West German students

demonstrated with placards reading 'Eden, Murderer of Budapest'.

In the 1960s, United States' involvement in Vietnam determined that their government was in no moral position to denounce the USSR when Soviet troops moved into Czechoslovakia in 1968. Today, Soviet intervention in Afghanistan and influence in Poland mirror American actions in El Salvador and financial support of the former military dictatorship in Turkey.

The Cold War has also entailed the occupation of countries by foreign troops. In Britain, for example, where much is made of the fact that the country has not been invaded since 1066, 25,000 American troops are stationed at over 20 bases. There are 90,000 US troops in South Korea; by comparison, about 80,000 Russian soldiers are in Afghanistan. Map 7 of *The State of the World Atlas* brings out in telling visual ways the extent of occupation all over the contemporary world, and Korea provides a vivid demonstration of what an 'armed truce' can entail.[7] North Korea has a population of 18.4 million and maintains a military force totalling 780,000; South Korea, with a population of 38.7 million, has 600,000 troops. Expenditure is therefore being diverted from welfare to warfare.

Sometimes the division of Europe and the world has seemed less rigid than at others. From the mid-1950s Khrushchev was responsible for the policy known as 'peaceful co-existence'. There was a period of détente in the 1970s when Presidents Nixon and Brezhnev visited the other's countries and a range of commercial, technical and military agreements were signed. But always a period of relative relaxation has been followed by abuse and recriminations.

Part of the mythology of the Cold War holds that the other side is simply itching to embark upon a programme of belligerent expansion. In fact, what is far more striking is how carefully the United States and the Soviet Union have respected each other's spheres of influence.

Take the Soviet Union, which if one looks at the postwar balance sheet has been remarkably unsuccessful if it is to be judged in terms of territorial gain—both Yugoslavia and Albania have detached themselves from the Soviet orbit, and Rumania insists on an independent foreign policy. China is also an unfriendly power situated on a vulnerable Soviet frontier. Second, the behaviour of Stalin was thoroughly cautious towards 'Western' Europe in the late 1940s: he sent no aid to the Greek communists in the civil war there, and reined back the Italian and French Communist Parties. Why? Because France, Italy and Greece were 'American', and Stalin knew full well that the United States would brook no substantial interference.

Next, in the Third World Soviet military assistance and other forms of aid, especially in Latin America, has been meagre. As Mary Kaldor has written, 'in general, Soviet advisers have been strictly segregated from local politicians and Soviet aid has even been extended to governments which persecute the Communist Party.' It was also the Soviet Union which backed down over the Cuban Missile Crisis in October 1962; and finally, Dr Paul Smoker, in a paper read at the British Association for the Advancement of Science conference in 1983, showed that the United States had intervened militarily in 64 conflicts between 1945 and 1976, the Soviet Union in six. None of these points squares with the traditional picture of an omnivorous Soviet Union. To argue this, contrary to established Cold War orthodoxy, is not in any way to revile or applaud Soviet domestic policy.[8]

Similarly, when looking at the United States, one sees an enormous quantity of rhetoric and frenzy whenever there are risings within the Eastern bloc—East Germany 1953, Hungary 1956, Czechoslovakia 1968, Poland from 1980—and perhaps some sanctions are imposed, but that is as far as it goes. Why? Because successive American administrations know full well that the Soviet Union would brook no substantial interference here.

In fact for both powers the Cold War is a useful mechanism for intimidating and keeping in line their own domestic populations. How easy it is to divert attention away from 'little local difficulties' by launching verbal assaults on 'the other' and playing the patriotic card 'the homeland in danger' in order to secure a spurious, temporary but effective 'national unity'. Dissent can be brushed off as 'unAmerican' or 'anti-Soviet'.

It also means that international incidents are played up for all they are worth. The Soviet intervention in Afghanistan in December 1979 followed on from NATO's decision a fortnight earlier to introduce a new range of nuclear weapons. The shooting down of the South Korean airliner on 1 September 1983 supplies a useful justification for an increased military budget. The *Times* carried this report on 17 September 1983:

> The House of Representatives, in the wake of the Korean airline disaster, yesterday gave final congressional approval by 266 votes to 152 to a $187,500 million defence authorization Bill for 1984. The Bill ends a 15-year US ban on production of chemical weapons. It also authorizes the production of the first 21 giant MX nuclear missiles which the President has said are essential for his arms modernization programmes in the face of the Soviet military build-up.

All of this follows on from the decisions and choices made during the crucial decade of the 1940s. And yet the early 1940s indicated that it need not have been like this.

What is the situation if one narrows the focus and concentrates on Britain? What can the people in this country do to reverse the Cold War assumption of the priority of military expenditure over welfare? What are the obstacles in the way of progressive change, and how do they compare with the forces for change?

The context after the June 1983 election is bleak. Mrs Thatcher's Conservative Party was returned to power with a large majority, and her opponents are having to respond to an agenda drawn up by the Convervatives. The Labour Party vote was the lowest since 1918, and in real terms it was the worst performance in its history – this in a country where four million people are without a job. Barely one in three trade unionists voted Labour, only 17 per cent of new voters and less than half the unemployed. Polls indicated that every policy of the Conservatives, bar that on the health service, was more appealing than that of their opponents. Labour Party membership is the lowest it has been for 50 years, and trade union membership has dropped one-and-a-half million since the end of 1979.

The malaise goes even deeper than this survey suggests, because the election campaign demonstrated yet again the lack of political and social consciousness in Britain. Holiday tour operators reported a doubling of bookings in early June as people fled the election. A poll in the *Times* showed that few politicians attracted widescale public recognition; a third of those interviewed either did not know that Norman Tebbit was a Conservative or thought he was a member of another party. Another survey in 1982 revealed that when a sample of people were asked to place 23 aspects of social life in order of preference, politics came last—lower than religion. Without romanticizing the 1940s the contrast is clear, as chapter 3 indicated; lacking a certain level of political interest or awareness the foundations for change will be flimsy indeed.

Second, the election demonstrated once again the sophistication of Conservative campaigning. It may be brash, showbiz stuff but it seems to work. In fact the Conservatives have invariably led the way in communicating with the electorate, as they did in the 1930s (see chapter 2). In the 1950s opinion polls were shaping their approach to the public, and the high-pressure advertising firm Saatchi and Saatchi was hired in the 1970s not merely to boost the Conservatives' own image but to undermine that of the Labour Party.

In the election campaign of May—June 1983, the Conservatives once more called the shots, using word processors, up-to-date computers and direct mail advertising to two million target voters, concentrating on 100 key marginal seats and setting up a 24-hour monitoring unit. They had at least £5 million to finance such activities. The Labour Party lacked all of this and—one telling comparison—now has just 63 agents.

Another obstacle lies in mass unemployment, and—as in the 1930s—the apathy and fear that this can bring in its wake. Sometimes it does indeed appear that 'there is no alternative'. A survey by the trade union NALGO early in 1983 of a 'sympathetic sample' found that 'The state of the nation is accepted with resignation and seen as an inevitability about which little can or could have been done.' Unemployment can also lead to racial tensions. The *Economist* of 17—23 September 1983 commented on the 'Europe-wide resentment against immigrants that has intensified as Europe-wide unemployment has risen'.

A fourth obstacle is the media. The tabloid press in particular is unremitting in its campaign against selected individuals such as Tony Benn, Ken Livingstone and Peter Tatchell, and against the Labour Party and trade unions; the return of the epithet 'Red' is another indication of the worsening Cold War. Since 1979 Mrs˙ Thatcher has knighted the editors of the *Sun*, and the *Daily Mail* and the *Sunday Express*, and the proprietor of the *Daily Express* and the *Star* has been created a peer. Television is in general more 'balanced', but even there studies by the Glasgow University Media Group have showed up distortions and, above all, omissions.

What is termed the 'military-industrial complex' — that is, the interlocking of the armed forces, arms manufacturers and establishment personnel — has now developed a momentum of its own. The *Financial Times* of 21 April 1981, reporting on American defence contractors, showed that firms such as General Dynamics and the McDonnell Corporation receive government awards totalling billions of dollars a year — they clearly have an interest in the escalation of the arms race. In Britain the Ministry of Defence orders more than £5,000 million of equipment and services from private industry each year, and the Falklands War is estimated to have launched a £1,000 million boom in the British defence sector. Firms like British Aerospace, Plessey and Racal have assets worth millions of pounds tied up in this area and would doubtless defend those interests if they were threatened by massive armaments cuts.[9]

Another obstacle to change lies in the continuity of so many British institutions, whether it be the monarchy, the Civil Service or the House of Lords. Like the Catholic Church, these bodies have seen many different governments, political parties and individuals come and go, and they are adept at damping down or diverting pressure for change.

Finally, the labour movement itself has become marginalized and fragmented. Anyone who has been out canvassing door-to-door during 1983 knows of the abuse hurled at trade unions and their leaders, the 'back to Moscow' remarks and the slander of minority groups. As mentioned earlier, Labour Party and trade union membership is declining and none of the other groups on 'the left' number more than a few thousand — and usually no more than tens or hundreds. Often activity consists of small meetings in which like-minded people debate issues which necessitate a further meeting or the formulation of a new committee.

In sum these obstacles are enormous, and it is episodes such as the Falklands War which demonstrate that when several of the above factors coincide, the results can be seismic and long-term in effect.

How about the forces for change? In December 1979 NATO announced the future deployment of a new range of nuclear weapons, and the reaction to this decision was much more powerful than anyone could have foreseen. CND was revitalized and the subsequent marches, demonstrations and media coverage have been far larger than in the 1950s and early 1960s. The campaign has been strengthened by its international dimensions, with a sizeable movement in West Germany and Holland, and the 'freeze' protest in the United States. Many adults and young people have been drawn into anti-nuclear activities who might normally have continued happily on their 'apolitical' way.

But even here there are drawbacks. The Conversative Party in Britain is regarding, however spuriously, its election victory as a mandate for the introduction of Cruise missiles. CND also spawned the campaign for European Nuclear Disarmament which has attempted to establish links with the unofficial peace campaigners in Eastern Europe. The government in response has played up the old 'them' and 'us' division — with Michael Heseltine, the British defence minister, smearing CND as Moscow-directed; the fact that there is no evidence for this claim appears quite immaterial.

Another optimistic change in the last few years has been the growing awareness and strength of formerly ignored groups of people such as women, blacks and gays. In every case organizations, meeting-places, magazines and books have been set up, and some kind of 'voice' established. However, a Britain in recession has led to increasing intolerance and discrimination.

To compare the forces for progressive change with the obstacles and drawbacks is to gain some idea of the massive task ahead: the task of constructing a coalition of, say, 50 per cent of the British people that will lead to the implementation of measures for a more just and equitable society. Thus the coalition will have to embrace figures as diverse as David Steel, Frank Chapple and Arthur Scargill. Laughable? No, for this is exactly the kind of consensus which was built during the war and ensured that even the proposals of a rather staid Liberal ex-civil servant like Beveridge sound mildly revolutionary today.

The circumstances of the 1940s and the 1980s are very different, and it can never be a case of merely transplanting techniques and approaches from then to now. Of course much of the wartime radicalism was fuelled by the war. Today any major war is likely to be nuclear or may even, as with the Falklands conflict, witness a reinforcement of conservatism. But to look at the 1940s is to see that it can be done, that radical and socialist values can occupy the mainstream of British life and shift the Conservative Party out to the periphery.

It is therefore important that a rather different 'popular memory' should be emphasized, and here the 1940s are vital. Instead of allowing the war and its immediate aftermath to be confiscated by Mrs Thatcher and others of her persuasion in terms of Churchillian rhetoric, it should be argued again and again that this is a complete distortion. No one is saying that many Conservatives did not fight hard and die bravely in the war — far from it — but that it was an anti-fascist war in which radical moods and beliefs prevailed.

One vital need is to rebuild a political culture so that 'politics' is no longer a dirty word or an instant conversation-stopper. This will entail dispensing with slogans and easy answers, and instead trying to communicate and educate in clear, accessible ways. There can be no greater contrast than between books such as *Tory MP*, *Why You Should be a Socialist*, *Guilty Men*, *Your MP*, *The Trial of Mussolini*, *Why Not Trust the Tories?* and others published by Gollancz and Penguin Specials in the 1930s and 1940s, and many of the 'left' books today which use specialized and elitist language. It is a question not so much of writing for and appealing to those already in the know, but of reaching out much wider than that. The word 'popularize' is often thought to have many repellent connotations — Hollywood, the tabloid press and all that — but the labour movement must in effect popularize its ideas and values.

New forms of communication have to be created and developed. The labour movement is still fixated by a 'print culture', and although printed words can still play a useful role (like this book?!), television is the most potent means of communication in modern Britain. Shouldn't the labour movement be considering the establishment of a radio station, a cable company or a television station rather than, as they are today, planning to spend nearly £7 million on a daily newspaper?

Furthermore, the sweeping economic and social changes which have occurred in this country since the war must be recognized and faced head on. Traditional industries such as steel, mining, engineering, shipbuilding and cars are in decline along with the proportion of manual labourers. They are being replaced by the new service and information concerns. Areas where the Labour Party could count on solid support—council estates, manual labour, the public sector, the regional heartlands and the inner city—are suffering badly in the recession, and new groups of people are coming to the fore who have no 'labourist' background, like white-collar, professional, service and managerial workers.

The growth of home entertainment has led to the fading away of the public meeting. Factors such as the decline of city centres and public transport and the spread of central heating make the home increasingly attractive, and television, hi-fi, electronic games, the prospect of home shopping and banking via cable have lessened the necessity to venture into the city. There are also now 12 million home owners, a rise of 6 million since 1960. None of these changes diminishes in any way the imperative for a powerful labour movement, but they do mean that if it is to be relevant and, more importantly, to be felt to be relevant by the people themselves, then changes and rethinking are required.

This ties in with the obligation to create new, viable options and alternatives. In the 1940s these centred around public ownership and the welfare state, but today, whilst defending these gains, it is important to push forward and initiate concrete proposals relating to workers' control and production for need and not profit—here the experience of the Lucas Aerospace shop stewards is vital. Similarly, as regards the whole issue of defence and nuclear weapons, new forms of non-nuclear defence must be discussed and publicized, a good start being the proposals of the Alternative Defence Commission published early in 1983 as *Defence Without the Bomb*.[10]

Many of Britain's institutions are now under intense pressure—the legal system is perhaps the most notable case. Periodicals like the *Economist*, in its issue of 30 July—5 August 1983, point up the defects of 'the mother of parliaments':

> As far as control of the executive is concerned—whatever the textbooks may say—the House of Commons is no more significant than a somewhat unruly press conference. Not merely unruly: the House is usually less efficient in eliciting information and often less effective in checking ministers than an ordinary press conference would be.

Now is the time to put forward specific and detailed plans which would both show up the limitations of almost all our long-hallowed institutions and illustrate ways in which they can be democratized and made more accountable to public scrutiny.

All of these suggestions can be argued for convincingly only if the aura of wheeling and dealing which does cling to the labour movement in the public eye is done away with. It is vital that the movement becomes the unflinching proponent of democratic practices and ideas—which will mean facing up to such changes as proportional representation, the end of the trade union block vote, regular and open elections of trade union officials and one-member one-vote in Labour Party contests. This is not a matter of expediency, and in fact the short term may well see some apparent defeats, but there is no way lasting change can be implemented if it is based on the trading off of interests in what are the now famous 'smoke-filled rooms'. The overwhelming stress on democracy should also be supplemented by plans to increase 'liberty', with a Freedom of Information Act and the open accountability of the police, armed forces and secret service.

The labour and peace movements should not be afraid to talk about values, to counter Mrs Thatcher's appeal to the supposedly Victorian values of greed and 'I'm all right, Jack' individualism with those of justice, friendship and equality. Admittedly not too much behaviour within the Labour Party and trade unions lives up to these standards, but then that is another priority. A long series of polls has shown that an institution like the National Health Service does still attract overwhelming public support and the values of the NHS at its best—of need before payment—are exactly those which must underlie any proposals.

Nor can these ideas develop in isolation, away from the mainstream of public life. Members of the Liberal Party and the SDP should stop being written off as 'beyond the pale' or not even worth establishing a dialogue with—it is not as if the labour movement is at present so gorged with success that it can afford not to examine and debate every option. Dialogue does at least offer the prospect of progress; the ostrich with its head in the sand offers no prospect of anything.

All these suggestions will entail a drastic rethinking of many attitudes and activities which are now 'taken for granted'. But it is precisely because they *are* taken for granted, and the forces for change are so weak, that now is the time for such rethinking to take place.

But enveloping all this, the parameters in which everything takes place, is that terrible hangover from the 1940s—the Cold War, which has split and paralysed so many fruitful plans and initiatives. It is a matter of supreme urgency that the division of Germany and Europe should begin to be healed, because, without the lessening of this tension, any change is likely to remain superficial or be shortlived—just as the radical momentum unleashed by the anti-fascist war was destroyed by the onset of the Cold War.

A guide to reading

Often books include a bibliography at the end which turns out to be no more than endless lists of titles – a testament to the author's diligence but of little help in distinguishing the useful from the useless.

This guide picks out some of the material available, and obviously it is very selective. For instance it concentrates almost exclusively on books – several useful articles are noted in the references. Some books, especially biographies, straddle a number of chapters and so I have mentioned them where most appropriate. The dates refer to the editions I used, and most of the books have been published in paperback.

A.J.P.Taylor's *English History 1914 – 1945* (London: Penguin 1970) contains a valuable bibliographical section, and Roger Eatwell's *The Labour Governments 1945 – 1951* (London: Batsford 1979) has suggestions for the later period.

General

It can take months to go through a run of newspapers, as well as ruining your eyesight. I used the *Times*, which has an index, the *Economist* and the *Daily Worker*. As for periodicals, the little-known *Pilot Papers* was fascinating, together with the *New Statesman* and the cultural *Our Time*.

The cabinet papers, when released under the 30-year rule, are available in the Public Record Office at Kew. Worth visiting as they have a speedy indexing system.

Diaries and correspondence often provide telling details or asides. I drew upon Mathilde Wolff-Monckeberg's *On the Other*

Side (London: Pan 1982); Frank Thompson's *There is a Spirit* (London: Gollancz 1947); George Orwell's *Collected Essays, Journalism and Letters* in four volumes (London: Penguin 1970); and Janina David's moving *A Square of Sky* and *A Touch of Earth*, in one volume (London: Penguin 1981). All of the books published by Mass-Observation during the 1940s are invaluable, particularly *War Factory* (London: Gollancz 1943), *Peace and the Public* (London: Longmans 1947) and *Puzzled People* (London: Gollancz 1947).

There are countless novels set during the war, ranging from Olivia Manning's marvellous *The Balkan Trilogy* and *The Levant Trilogy* (all six in Penguin), to Evelyn Waugh's dull *Sword of Honour* trilogy (Penguin). Some of Anthony Powell's *A Dance to the Music of Time* sequence (Fontana) cover the 1940s, and Alexander Baron's *From the City, From the Plough* (St Albans: Mayflower 1979) is worth a read. There are of course George Orwell's novels, and also Rex Warner's *The Aerodrome* (Oxford University Press 1982). I could make little headway with Edward Upward's trilogy *The Spiral Ascent* (London: Heinemann 1977). The Oasis Trust have recently published two volumes of soldiers' poetry.

As for paintings, the War Artists' Advisory Committee commissioned many works, the best-known being Henry Moore's tube shelter drawings. The films of this time are also evocative, especially those of the Crown Film Unit and Ealing Studios—for the latter see Charles Barr's illuminating *Ealing Studios* (London: Cameron and Tayleur 1977). Roberto Rossellini's trilogy *Rome, Open City* (1945), *Paisan* (1946) and *Germany, Year Zero* (1947) are moving, but most terrifying of all are the Soviet frontline documentaries filmed by absurdly brave cameramen, many of whom were killed in the process.

1. All our yesterdays?

There are a number of good books on popular memory, such as Paul Fussell's *The Great War and Modern Memory* (Oxford University Press 1975), Philip Knightley's *The First Casualty* (London: Quartet 1978), with information on the war correspondent as myth-maker, and Tom Harrisson's *Living Through the Blitz* (London: Penguin 1978). Nicholas Harman's *Dunkirk* (London: Coronet 1981) has numerous insights, as does James Margach's broader *The Abuse of Power* (London: Star 1979). Ian McLaine's *Ministry of Morale* (London: Allen & Unwin 1979) is informative if a little stodgy, and Henry Tudor's *Political Myth* (London: Pall Mall 1972) unhelpful. Finally, useful introductions to the whole subject of history and perception are E.H.Carr's *What is History?* (London: Penguin 1974), John Berger's *Ways of Seeing* (London: Penguin 1972) and Colin McArthur's *Television and History* (London: British Film Institute 1978).

2. Britain and Europe in the Thirties

Taylor's *English History* (mentioned above) is solid, and C.L.Mowat's *Britain Between the Wars 1918–1940* (London: Methuen 1955) stimulating. Branson and Heinemann's *Britain in the Nineteen Thirties* (St Albans: Panther 1973) is a good book, and Julian Symons's *The Thirties* (London: Faber 1975) very readable. There is a fine essay by John Saville called 'May day 1937' in the *Essays in Labour History 1918–1939* (London: Croom Helm 1977) which he edited with Asa Briggs. Ben Pimlott's *Labour and the Left in the 1930s* (Cambridge: Cambridge University Press 1976) is provocative and Bernard Crick's *George Orwell* (London: Penguin 1982) exhaustive.

For matters abroad, there is a whole clutch of biographies about Hitler. Also invaluable are Isaac Deutscher's *Stalin* (London: Penguin 1966) and Fernando Claudin's *The Communist Movement* (London: Penguin 1975). Two contrasting views of the Spanish Civil War are Broue and Temine's *The Revolution and the Civil War in Spain* (London: Faber 1972) and Hugh Thomas's *The Spanish Civil War* (London: Penguin 1977).

3. Britain during the war

There are numerous books which cover this subject, but two are indispensable: Angus Calder's *The People's War* (London: Panther 1971) and Paul Addison's *The Road to 1945* (London: Quartet 1977).

Norman Longmate's *How We Lived Then* (London: Arrow 1973) is an immensely detailed history of everyday life. Another useful study is Susan Brigg's *Keep Smiling Through* (London: Weidenfeld & Nicolson 1975). Three rather superficial books are Richard Collier's *1940: The World in Flames* (London: Penguin 1980), Laurence Thompson's *1940* (London: Collins 1966) and Constantine FitzGibbon's *The Blitz* (London: MacDonald 1970). Despite its dull title, a tremendous book — which should be reprinted — is Richard Titmuss's *Problems of Social Policy* (London: HMSO 1950). Contemporary books and collections worth a look at are: 'Cato's' *Guilty Men* (London: Gollancz 1940), Ritchie Calder's *Carry On London* (London: Universities' Press 1941) and *The Lesson of London* (London: Secker & Warburg 1941), J.B.Priestley's *Postscripts* broadcasts, Churchill's speeches and the ITMA radio programmes, some of which scripts are in *The ITMA Years* (London: Futura 1975). For foreign policy, look at Elisabeth Barker's *Churchill and Eden at War* (London: Macmillan 1978).

4. The war in Europe

A useful introduction is B.H.Liddell Hart's *History of the Second World War* (London: Cassell 1970). Alexander Werth's *Russia at War 1941 – 1945* (London: Pan 1965) is fittingly on an epic scale. Perceptive and wide-ranging is James D.Wilkinson's *The Intellectual Resistance in Europe* (USA: Harvard 1981). As for the Resistance, there is M.R.D.Foot's standard *Resistance* (London: Paladin 1978), *Resistance in Europe: 1939 – 45* (London: Penguin 1976) edited by S.Hawes and R.White, and the contemporary *Europe Rises* (London: Gollancz 1943) by Dorothy Woodman. Ian Grey's *Stalin* (London: Abacus 1982) is provoking. There is a whole clutch of superb books on Yugoslavia and Greece during the war: Fitzroy Maclean's *Eastern Approaches* (London: Cape 1949), F.W.D.Deakin's *The Embattled Mountain* (London: Oxford University Press 1971), Basil Davidson's *Special Operations Europe* (London: Gollancz 1980), Milovan Djilas's *Wartime* (London: Secker & Warburg 1977), S.Sarafis's *ELAS* (London: Merlin 1981) and the book edited by R.Clogg and P.Auty called *British*

Policy towards Wartime Resistance in Yugoslavia and Greece (London: Macmillan 1975).

5. The aftermath

Many of the books mentioned above and below are relevant here, but also look at William Harrington and Peter Young's *The 1945 Revolution* (London: Davis-Poynter 1978). Although slightly later, *The Railway* (London: British-Yugoslav Association 1948), edited by E.P.Thompson, conveys some of the optimism of the period.

6. Britain in the late Forties

Eatwell's *The Labour Governments 1945 – 1951* (London: Batsford 1981) is a good start, particularly if read alongside the essays in *Age of Austerity 1945 – 1951* (London: Penguin 1963) edited by Michael Sissons and Philip French. Robert Brady's *Crisis in Britain* (USA: University of California Press 1950) is encyclopaedic, and A.Rogow and Peter Shore's *The Labour Governments and British Industry 1945 – 1951* (Oxford: Blackwell 1955) informative. Michael Foot's *Aneurin Bevan 1945 – 1960* (London: Paladin 1975) is powerful and partisan, reflecting the subject's character, as do the biographies of *Herbert Morrison*, by B.Donoghue and G.W.Jones (London: Weidenfeld & Nicolson 1973) and of *Attlee* by Kenneth Harris (London: Weidenfeld & Nicolson 1983). There are numerous studies of the Labour Party, such as Ralph Miliband's *Parliamentary Socialism* (London: Merlin 1972), David Coates's *The Labour Party and the Struggle for Socialism* (Cambridge: Cambridge University Press 1975) and David Howell's *British Social Democracy* (London: Croom Helm 1980). As regards the Conservative Party, see Andrew Gamble's *The Conservative Nation* (London: Routledge 1974). Derek Fraser's *The Evolution of the British Welfare State* (London: Macmillan 1973) is a valuable starting point.

7. The making of Western Europe

A comprehensive, if rather sour, introduction is Howard Zinn's

A People's History of the United States (London: Longman 1980). David Horowitz's *From Yalta to Vietnam* (London: Penguin 1971) is essential, as are the essays he edited called *Corporations and the Cold War* (USA: Monthly Review Press 1970), Tom Nairn (ed.) *Atlantic Europe?* (Amsterdam: Transnational Institute 1976) and Carl Marzani's *We Can Be Friends* (USA: Topical Books 1952). As for Europe itself, Barbara Ward's *The West at Bay* (London: Allen & Unwin 1948) is perceptive. For France, there is Alexander Werth's *De Gaulle* (London. Penguin 1965), Philip Williams's immensely detailed *Politics in Post-War France* (London: Longman 1968) and the more readable *A History of Modern France 1871 – 1962* (London: Penguin 1965) by Alfred Cobban. For Italy, Elizabeth Wiskemann's *Italy Since 1945* (London: Macmillan 1971) is an introductory book, and Donald Sassoon's *The Strategy of the Italian Communist Party* (London: Frances Pinter 1981) is revealing but more specialized. Keith Middlemas's *Power and the Party* (London: Deutsch 1980) tackles the communist parties in Europe since the war.

8. The making of Eastern Europe

An introduction to this whole area of Europe is Robin Okey's *Eastern Europe 1740 – 1980* (London: Hutchinson 1980). Concerning the period itself, Doreen Warriner's *Revolution in Eastern Europe* (London: Turnstile 1950) is vital. For Poland, see Neal Ascherson's *The Polish August* (London: Penguin 1981), and a more personal account of the postwar Czechoslovakia is Marion Slingova's *Truth Will Prevail* (London: Merlin 1968). Milovan Djilas's *Conversations with Stalin* (London: Penguin 1964) is important as are Vladimir Dedijer's *Tito Speaks* (London: Weidenfeld & Nicolson 1953) and Phyllis Auty's marvellous *Tito* (London: Penguin 1974). Hugh Seton-Watson's *The Pattern of Communist Revolution* (London: Methuen 1960) is a typical 'Cold War' account.

9. The Cold War

Many of the books mentioned above also cover this subject.

Elisabeth Barker's *The Cold War* (London: Wayland 1972) is a brief introduction. Basil Davidson's *Germany: What Now?* (London: Muller 1950) deserves to be much better known. Tom Bower's *Blind Eye to Murder* (London: Paladin 1982) demonstrates the flaws of the Allies' 'denazification' programme and contrasts with Gordon Schaffer's *Russian Zone* (London: Allen & Unwin 1947). Bill Jones's *The Russia Complex* (Manchester University Press 1977) is over-impressed with the virtues of power politics. Two very contrasting books are Wilfred Burchett's *Cold War in Germany* (Australia: Unity 1950) and Richard Collier's *Bridge Across the Sky* (London: Magnum 1980).

10. Forty years on

Obviously there is a huge volume of material available on events since the 1940s. Regarding Britain, Keith Middlemas's *Politics in Industrial Society* (London: Deutsch 1979) is solid and very serious, in contrast to the rather skimpy *Post-War Britain* (London: Penguin 1979) by Alan Sked and Chris Cook and Arthur Marwick's *British Society Since 1945* (London: Penguin 1982). Two collections of essays, *The Age of Affluence* (London: Macmillan 1970) edited by V.Bogdanor and R.Skidelsky and *The Decade of Distinction* (London: Macmillan 1972) edited by D.McKie and C.Cook, are variable in quality. John Westergaard and Henrietta Resler's *Class in a Capitalist Society* (London: Penguin 1976) is factual and argumentative, whilst Andrew Gamble's *Britain in Decline* (London: Papermac 1981) is a thoughtful study. A.H.Halsey's *Change in British Society* (Oxford: Oxford University Press 1981) is helpful, and Christopher Harvie's history of modern Scotland, *No Gods and Precious Few Heroes* (London: Edward Arnold 1981), is pessimistic but excellent. Paul Foot's *The Politics of Harold Wilson* (London: Penguin 1968) is characteristically biting. Anthony Sampson's anatomies of Britain are useful social-democratic surveys—the latest edition being *The Changing Anatomy of Britain* (London: Hodder & Stoughton 1982). Finally, E.P.Thompson's collections *Writing By Candlelight* (London: Merlin 1980) and *Zero Option* (London: Merlin 1982) are stimulating.

For Europe, Mary Kaldor's *The Disintegrating West* (London: Penguin 1979) is an intriguing introduction, as is Fred Halliday's recent *The Making of the Second Cold War* (London: Verso 1983). Alfred Grosser's *The Western Alliance* (London: Papermac 1980) is disappointing. Eastern Europe is covered in François Fejto's *A History of the People's Democracies* (London: Penguin 1974). More personal accounts are by V.Micunovic in *Moscow Diary* (London: Chatto & Windus 1980) dealing with Hungary in 1956, and Z.Mlynar's *Night Frost in Prague* (London: Hurst 1978) on Czechoslovakia, 1968. As regards Poland, see Neal Ascherson's *The Polish August* (chapter 8 above) and Martin Myant's *Poland: A Crisis for Socialism* (London: Lawrence & Wishart 1982). Pluto Press publish an annual *World View* which provides a comprehensive chronology and guide to the past year's events, together with some interpretative essays.

I should emphasize that this guide does no more than scrape the surface of what is on offer, and I would be very pleased to provide further suggestions to anyone who cares to get in touch with me, c/o Pluto Press, The Works, 105A Torriano Avenue, London NW5 2RX.

References

1. All our yesterdays?

1. Winston Churchill, *The Gathering Storm*, London: Cassell 1948, p.601.
2. *Atlantic Monthly*, September 1949, pp.35−44.
3. Philip Knightley, *The First Casualty*, London: Quartet 1978, pp.230−33; Nicholas Harman *Dunkirk*, London: Coronet 1980.
4. Ken Worpole, 'The popular literature of the Second World War' in his *Dockers and Detectives*, London: Verso 1983.
5. Bernard Crick, *George Orwell*, London: Secker & Warburg 1980, p.398.

2. Britain and Europe in the Thirties

1. Quoted in Ralph Miliband, *Parliamentary Socialism*, London: Merlin 1972, p.202.
2. Henry Pelling (ed), *A History of British Trade Unionism*, Harmondsworth: Penguin 1976, p.208.
3. Robert Blake, *The Conservative Party from Peel to Churchill*, London: Fontana 1972, p.236.
4. John Saville, *May Day 1937* in Asa Briggs and John Saville (eds), *Essays in Labour History 1918−1939*, London: Croom Helm 1977, p.239.
5. C.L.Mowat, *Britain Between the Wars*, London: Methuen, 1956, p.573.
6. Robert Rhodes James, *Churchill: A Study in Failure 1900−1939*, Harmondsworth: Pelican 1973, pp.291−92. James is today a Conservative MP.
7. James Margach, *The Abuse of Power*, London: Star 1979, p.53.

8. See for example Simon Haxey, *Tory MP*, London: Gollancz 1939 and the more recent Richard Griffiths, *Fellow-Travellers of the Right*, London: Constable 1980.
9. 'Cato', *Guilty Men*, London: Gollancz 1940, p.78.

3. Britain during the war

1. Nigel Hamilton, *Monty: The Making of a General*, Feltham: Hamlyn Paperback 1981, p.344.
2. Richard Collier, *1940: The World in Flames*, Harmondsworth: Penguin 1980, p.15.
3. Richard Titmuss, *Problems of Social Policy*, London: HMSO 1950, p.516.
4. Paul Addison, *The Road to 1945*, London: Quartet 1977, p.72.
5. Constantine FitzGibbon, *The Blitz*, London: MacDonald 1970, p.26.
6. Ritchie Calder, *Carry On London*, London: English Universities Press 1941, p.53.
7. C.FitzGibbon, *The Blitz*, p.84.
8. Mary Stocks, *The Workers' Educational Association: The First 50 Years*, London: Allen & Unwin 1953, p.124.
9. Figures in D.Stark Murray, *Why a National Health Service?*, London: Pemberton 1970, and the two chapters on the war.
10. George Orwell, *My Country Right or Wrong*, vol. 2, *Collected Essays, Journalism and Letters*, Harmondsworth: Penguin 1970, p.141.
11. Janet Minihan, *The Nationalization of Culture*, London: Hamish Hamilton 1977, p.220.
12. See Ann Lindsay, *The Theatre*, London: Bodley Head 1948.
13. Letter by Sir Tom Hopkinson in the *Times* of 8 January 1980. Also see the two-volume *Since 1939*, London: Phoenix House 1949.
14. Quoted by Henry Pelling in 'The 1945 general election reconsidered' in *The Historical Journal*, vol.23 no.2 (1980), p.400.
15. Keith Middlemas, *Politics in Industrial Society*, London: Deutsch 1979, p.275.
16. J.T.Murphy, *Victory Production!*, London: Bodley Head 1942, pp.63—4.
17. Calder, *Carry on London*, p.160.
18. *Tribune*, 4 December 1942.

19. See D.L.Prynn, 'Common Wealth' in *Journal of Contemporary History*, vol.7 nos.1−2, January−April 1972, pp.169−79.
20. Tom Harrisson 'Public opinion about Russia' in *The Political Quarterly*, vol.XII no.4, October−December 1941, p.365; and J.T.Murphy, *Victory Production!*, pp.86−7.

4. The war in Europe

1. See for example Michael Padev, *Marshall Tito*, London: Muller 1944.
2. 'Symmachos', *Greece Fights On*, London: Drummond no date, pp.70−1.
3. Roland Penrose, *In the Service of the People*, London: Heinemann 1945, p.56.
4. Ian Grey, *Stalin*, London: Abacus 1982, p.330.
5. B.H.Liddell Hart, *History of the Second World War*, London: Cassell 1970, p.478.
6. Frida Knight, *The French Resistance*, London: Lawrence & Wishart 1975, p.113.
7. See the references in the Guide to Reading.
8. Stefano Sarafis, *ELAS*, London: Merlin 1980.
9. Penrose, *In the Service of the People*, pp.54−5.
10. Dorothy Woodman, *Europe Rises*, London: Gollancz 1943, p.18.
11. Winston Churchill, *Triumph and Tragedy*, London: Cassell, p.198.
12. Winston Churchill, *Triumph and Tragedy*, p.252. Also Michael Foot, *Aneurin Bevan 1897−1945*, St Albans: Paladin 1975, pp.476−89.
13. Parnell's *History of the Second World War*, p.1783.
14. Field Marshall Montgomery, *Memoirs*, London: Collins 1958, p.454.

5. The aftermath

1. Alexander Werth, *Russia at War*, London: Pan 1965, p.799.
2. Tom Driberg, *Ruling Passions*, London: Quartet 1978, pp.212−13.
3. Frank Thompson, *There is a Spirit in Europe*, London: Gollancz 1948, p.169.
4. Mathilde Wolff-Monckeberg, *On the Other Side*,

London: Pan 1982, p.170.

5. Quoted in S.Hawes and R.White (eds), *Resistance in Europe: 1939—45*, Harmondsworth: Pelican 1976, p.22.
6. Arthur Calder-Marshall, *The Watershed*, London: Contact 1947, p.79.
7. Quoted by Frida Knight, *The French Resistance*, London: Lawrence & Wishart 1975, pp.211—12.
8. Neal Ascherson, *The Polish August*, Harmondsworth: Penguin 1981, pp.43—4.
9. Granville Eastwood, *Harold Laski*, Oxford: Mowbray 1977, p.130.
10. Hugh Dalton, *High Tide and After*, London: Muller 1962, p.3.
11. Alfred Grosser, *The Western Alliance*, London: Papermac 1980, p.52.

6. Britain in the late Forties

1. Herbert Morrison, *An Autobiography*, Watford: Odhams 1960, p.251.
2. Clement Attlee, *As It Happened*, London: Heinemann 1954, p.165.
3. This whole subject is discussed in detail in R.A.Dahl, 'Workers' control of industry and the British Labour Party', in *American Political Science Review*, vol.XLI, October 1947, pp.875—900.
4. E.Shinwell, *Lead With The Left*, London: Cassell 1981, p.131.
5. Many of the figures in this chapter are taken from the monumental work by Robert A.Brady, *Crisis in Britain*, London: Cambridge University Press 1950.
6. Geoffrey Crowther, 'British socialism on trial' in *Atlantic Monthly*, May 1949, p.27.
7. References in this paragraph are from A.A.Rogow and P.Shore, *The Labour Government and British Industry 1945—51*, Oxford: Blackwell 1955.
8. T.Barna, 'Those "fruitfully high" profits' in *Bulletin of Oxford University Institute of Statistics*, vol.II July—August 1949, pp.213—27. Also see statistics from book in note 9.
9. Dudley Seers, *The Levelling of Incomes since 1938*, Oxford: Blackwell 1951, p.31.
10. James Harvey and Katherine Hood, *The British State*, London: Lawrence & Wishart 1958, p.237.

11. There is a fierce and illuminating debate on the Labour government's educational policy in *History Workshop*, no.7, Spring 1979, pp.156—69.
12. Hugh Dalton, *High Tide and After*, London: Muller 1962, p.352.
13. James Margach, *The Abuse of Power*, London: Star 1979, p.86.
14. Tom Harrisson, 'British opinion moves towards a new synthesis' in *Public Opinion Quarterly*, vol.II no.3, Fall 1947, p.335.
15. Mass-Observation, *Peace and the Public*, London: Longmans 1947, p.13.
16. Herbert Morrison, *The Peaceful Revolution*, London: Allen & Unwin 1949, p.45.
17. Jeremy Seabrook, *What Went Wrong?*, London: Gollancz 1978, p.87.

7. The making of Western Europe

1. Correlli Barnett, *The Collapse of British Power*, London: Eyre Methuen 1972, p.592.
2. Elisabeth Barker, *The Cold War*, London: Wayland 1972, p.18.
3. Quoted in Ian Grey, *Stalin*, London: Abacus 1982, p.435.
4. Bill Jones, *The Russia Complex*, Manchester: University Press 1977, p.117.
5. Quoted in Alexander Werth, *De Gaulle*, Harmondsworth: Penguin 1965, p.170.
6. Fernando Claudin, *The Communist Movement*, Harmondsworth: Peregrine 1975, p.333.
7. Donald Sassoon, *The Strategy of the Italian Communist Party*, London: Frances Pinter 1981, p.59.
8. Scott Newton, 'How successful was the Marshall Plan? in *History Today*, vol.33, November 1983, p.12.
9. Howard Zinn, *A People's History of the United States*, London: Longman 1980, p.430.
10. Elisabeth Barker, *The Cold War*, p.48.
11. Claude Julien, in Tom Nairn (ed), *Atlantic Europe?*, Amsterdam: Transnational Institute 1976, p.8.
12. Geoffrey Warner, 'Belgium, France and Italy 1944—50 in *History Today*, vol.33, September 1983, p.13.

8. The making of Eastern Europe

1. Ian Grey, *Stalin*, London: Abacus 1982, p.426.
2. Chatham House Study Group, *British Security*, London: Royal Institute of International Affairs 1946, p.97.
3. Roy Medvedev, *Let History Judge*, London: Macmillan 1972, p.490.
4. Neal Ascherson, *The Polish August*, Harmondsworth: Penguin 1981, p.47.
5. Martin McCauley, 'The experiences of eastern and south-eastern Europe' in *History Today* vol.33, October 1983, pp.37—8.
6. Martin Myant, *Poland: A Crisis of Socialism*, London: Lawrence & Wishart 1982, p.29.
7. Chris Harman, *Revolution and Bureaucracy in Eastern Europe*, London: Pluto Press 1974, p.58.
8. Robin Okey, *Eastern Europe 1740—1980*, London: Hutchinson 1982, p.200. Also see Fernando Claudin, *The Communist Movement*, Harmondsworth: Peregrine 1975, pp.520—1.
9. Stanley Evans, *A Short History of Bulgaria*, London: Lawrence & Wishart 1960, p.203.
10. Marian Slingova, *Truth will Prevail*, London: Merlin 1968, pp.101—2.

9. The Cold War

1. Roger Pethybridge, 'The Soviet Union' *History Today*, vol.33, October 1983 , p.30.
2. Basil Davidson, *Germany: What Now?*, London: Frederick Muller 1950, pp.140—1.
3. Ruth Evans in Mathilde Wolff-Monckeberg, *On the Other Side*, London: Pan 1982, p.179.
4. Howard Goorney, *The Theatre Workshop Story*, London: Eyre Methuen 1981, p.142.
5. Quoted in Carl Marzani, *We can be friends*, New York: Topical Books 1952, p.335.
6. See the *Times*, 20 and 21 September 1983. Also the important John Loftus, *The Belarus Secret*, Harmondsworth: Penguin 1983.
7. See the article by Peter Weiler in *Diplomatic History*, vol.5 no.1, Winter 1981, pp.1—22.
8. *Observer*, 3 January 1982. Also David Leigh, *The Frontiers of*

Secrecy, London: Junction 1980, pp.218−24.

9. The fact of US funding is now well established: see the references to Sassoon and Warner in chapter 7. Also Joseph La Palombara, *The Italian Labor Movement*, USA: Ithaca 1957, and Richard Fletcher in *The CIA and the Labour Movement*, Nottingham: Spokesman 1977.

10. Anthony Sampson, *Macmillan*, Harmondsworth: Penguin 1968, pp.88.9.

11. See Peter Weiler's account of the dock strike in J.E.Cronin and J.Schneer (eds), *Social Conflict and the Political Order in Modern Britain*, London: Croom Helm 1982, pp.146−78.

12. Robert Strading, 'Shostakovich and the Soviet system, 1925−1975', in C.Norris (ed), *Shostakovich: the Man and his Music*, London: Lawrence & Wishart 1982, p.200.

13. Mass-Observation, *Peace and the Public*, London: Longmans 1947, p.20. Also their *Puzzled People*, London: Gollancz 1947.

14. See E.P.Thompson (ed), *The Railway*, London: British−Yugoslav Association 1947, and Basil Davidson's article on Yugoslav self-management in *New Society*, 7 December 1978.

15. The *Times* 4 January 1982.

16. Basil Davidson, *Germany: What Now?*, London: Frederick Muller, 1950, p.231.

17. Elisabeth Barker, *The Cold War*, London: Wayland 1972, pp.69−70.

10. Forty years on

1. Sir William Beveridge, *The Pillars of Security*, London: Allen & Unwin 1943, p.143.

2. The *Times*, 21 September 1983.

3. *Guardian*, 22 December 1980.

4. E.P.Thompson, *Writing by Candlelight*, London: Merlin 1980, p.263.

5. Several of the figures in this chapter relating to armaments expenditure come from Dan Smith and Ron Smith, *The Economics of Militarism*, London: Pluto Press 1983.

6. Veljko Micunovic, *Moscow Diary*, London: Chatto & Windus 1980, p.134.

7. Michael Kidron and Ronald Segal, *The State of the World Atlas*, London: Pan 1981.

Name index

Ariel Dorfman
Widows

A political novel set ostensibly in Nazi-occupied Greece, but which
could as well be Chile, Argentina, El Salvador or anywhere else
today where people are 'disappeared'. Already a best seller in
America, where it has been acclaimed as a 'masterpiece'.

'His beautifully understated tale is as powerful as it is moving'
Publishers Weekly

'Like any good Greek drama, this story is told about real characters
who live and breathe, but somehow the meanings that mount and
accrue around the action magnify everything beyond human
proportions and the reader is constantly aware of being in the
presence of universal truths.' Barbara Raskin

0 86104 723 0   hardback   £7.95
paperback published by Abacus

Alice Cook and Gwyn Kirk

Greenham Women Everywhere

Dreams, ideas and actions from the women's peace movement

The first women's peace camp was set up in September 1981 at
Greenham Common. It has been a major catalyst in the growth of
opposition, both in the UK and abroad, to the escalation of the
nuclear arms race. **Greenham Women Everywhere** describes the
dreams, nightmares and personal statements of some of the many
women who, faced with the nuclear threat, have made the difficult
transition from private anxiety to collective commitment. It shows
their determination, imagination and strength; it discusses the
response of the media and the importance of legal support; it asserts
a belief in non-violent direct action which has inspired a campaign
well beyond Greenham.
Greenham Women Everywhere is a book to be read by activists in
the peace movement, by feminists, and by all those concerned about
the urgent need for nuclear disarmament.

0 86104 726 5   20 photographs   paperback   £3.50

Dan Smith and Ron Smith
The Economics of Militarism

Half a year's world military spending costs more than a ten-year programme to meet basic food and health needs in poor countries. This book explains how and why military spending occurs. It examines the state interests which motivate it, the bureaucracies which administer it and the corporations which profit from it.,
The Economics of Militarism is a comprehensive introduction to the consequences of arms spending which also investigates the economic feasibility of disarmament.

0 86104 370 7   paperback   £2.95

Brian Easlea

Fathering the Unthinkable
Masculinity, scientists and the nuclear arms race

– Why does the arms race continue?

– Why do military-industrial-scientific complexes have such an
insatiable demand for new weapons systems?

– Why does science co-operate so readily with this process?

In a lucid survey of science from Francis Bacon's 'truly masculine
science' to Robert Oppenheimer's devastating 'baby', Brian Easlea
shows how the seventeenth-century scientific revolution already
contained the seeds of today's oppressive technologies. He argues
for a revaluation of masculine institutions and ideologies, so that
science does not remain the willing accessory to man's war on
'feminine' values.

'Valuable contribution . . . buy it for any budding scientists you
know.' *Peace News*

240 pages   0 86104 391 X   paperback   £5.95

Pluto books are available through your local bookshop. In case of
difficulty write to:

Pluto Press Limited,
Freepost, (no stamp required)
105a Torriano Avenue,
London NW5 1YP

To order, enclose a cheque/p.o. payable to Pluto Press to cover the
price of the book, plus 50p per book for postage and packing (£2.50
maximum). Requests for catalogues and other information should be
sent to the above address. Telephone: 01-482 1973.